CW01560689

'For sheer actuality, the ultimate o
happening, I have never seen anyth.   ᵤᵤᵣpass this account.'
    - *Evening Post, Port Elizabeth.*

'What it's like to escape a plane crash . . . full of amazing tales
of bravery.'
    - *Keith Bartels, Southend Evening Echo.*

'A vivid account of how he saw death, yet survived.'
    - *Watford Evening Echo.*

'A gripping and well-told story.' - *Sandton Chronicle.*

'It makes compelling reading.'
    - *Brian Brown, Natal Daily News.*

'Something few people have survived . . .
a remarkable human drama.'
    - *John Tucker, Pretoria News.*

'A remarkable and dramatic story of heroism and cowardice
and, above all, survival in the face of the most terrifying of
modern experiences . . . a vivid and dramatic account: one that
offers surprising insight into the way traumatic events affect our
lives.' - *David Raath, Johannesburg Citizen.*

EARL MOORHOUSE

WAKE UP, IT'S A CRASH

The Survivors' Stories

Bilbury Lane

Published by Bilbury Lane 2015

Copyright © Earl Moorhouse 2014
Earl Moorhouse has asserted his right under the
Copyright, Designs and Patents Act 1988 to be
identified as the author of this work.

Cover and book design:
Lynn Moorhouse, FRSA, ARPS.

Publication history:
First published David & Charles Ltd, UK 1980
and Jonathan Ball, South Africa 1980
Corgi edition (Transworld Publishers Ltd),
published London, UK 1982
Squire's Yard (Bilbury Lane Ltd) Kindle ebook
revised edition published 2013

ISBN: 978-0-9569073-6-3

Bilbury Lane is an imprint of
Bilbury Lane Limited Reg. No. 03849327
Registered Office: Blenheim House,
Henry Street, Bath, UK
www.squiresyard.co.uk

Dedication

This book is for my sons,
Garett Jon and Brendon Scott,
and for all those who took
the last flight of Lufthansa's
Boeing 747 *Hessen* out of Nairobi.

Author's Note

People who write are never satisfied. What has been written can always be improved, rearranged, or expressed more elegantly. In preparing this story about the world's first Boeing 747 jumbo jet crash for publication as an e-book and a new paperback edition, I have undertaken a complete revision and updating of the original printed book. The text has been corrected from beginning to end, and new sections have been added. This was done so I could complete the story of some events, which were still unfolding when the original book was published. Also, it has allowed me to describe more fully the long-term impact the air crash has had on survivors.

1 • *Fifty Names*

It was shortly before ten on Wednesday morning, November 20, 1974, and already the South African sun was blazing down on the traffic rolling along the motorway leading to Johannesburg's international airport.

It was a beautiful morning, and for Johannesburg residents Patricia and Ian Horsfield and their three-year-old son Timothy, it was a happy day. They were driving to the airport to meet Ian's sister, her husband and two sons, who had spent the last three months in Europe.

The return of Ian's sister and her family was something of a surprise to the Horsfields. The original plan had been for the family to fly directly from Europe to Nairobi, in Kenya, where Earl Moorhouse, husband of Ian's sister, was due to start a new job. But there had been some difficulty involving their air tickets, and yesterday Earl had telephoned from Frankfurt, in Germany.

"Can you pick us up at the airport in the morning?" Earl had asked. "We can't get off in Nairobi, so we're coming straight through to Johannesburg."

"No problem at all," Ian had said. "I'll take the day off. They owe me a few anyway."

So now they travelled along steadily, cresting a hill, and saw the flat expanse of the airport in the distance. Ian noticed something briefly in his mirror, and a large American car roared past, buffeting the slower moving Horsfields.

As they drew into the airport car park they saw the car again. It was pulling into a parking space. The driver leaped out and ran wildly, dodging through the traffic, before disappearing into the airport building. The Horsfields shook their heads, laughing. They got out of their car, took young Timothy by the hand and strolled over to the international terminal.

Inside the building, they searched the arrivals indicator board for Flight LH540 from Frankfurt. The flight was not listed.

Ian Horsfield swore quietly. "There's no damned plane there," he said. "The bloody Moorhouses must have been talking about tomorrow. And I've gone and taken the day off."

They stood checking the changing letters. Perhaps the flight details would still appear.

But they did not.

Ian said, "Let's go and ask at the information

counter."

They walked over to the long desk on the international concourse. The woman working behind it looked up.

"Wasn't there supposed to be a Lufthansa flight arriving today?" Ian asked.

"Yes, there was," the woman said in a flat voice, "but it's been delayed."

"What do you mean, delayed? For how long?"

"Indefinitely."

"Indefinitely? What for?"

The Horsfields looked at each other, puzzled.

"Is there something wrong somewhere?" Ian asked. "Has something happened?"

"No," the woman said. "Look, why don't you phone Lufthansa? I don't know anything about it." She wrote down the number of the airline's office in central Johannesburg on a piece of paper and handed it to them.

They looked round, saw a bank of public telephones nearby and went over. Ian picked up a handset, looked at the piece of paper and began dialling. The number was engaged. He tried again. Engaged.

He was dialling a third time when two men came walking towards them, one with a camera slung from his neck.

"Excuse me," one said. "I'm from *Die Vaderland*."

"Oh, yes?" Ian looked at him.

"Were you waiting for someone on the Lufthansa flight?"

Ian felt himself go cold. He heard Patricia cry out, "Oh God, no. Oh, no."

He said to the newsman, "What's happened?"

"Well . . . " the man hesitated. "Look, can I have an interview with you?"

"I'm not interested in an interview," Ian said. "What's happened? Has there been an accident?"

The newsman looked at Patricia, then back at Ian. "Can I speak to you alone?"

"It's all right," Ian said, "you can speak in front of my wife. Has it crashed?"

"Yes." The newsman seemed troubled, and shook his head. "At Nairobi. We just heard that it had crashed. We don't . . . "

"How bad?"

The reporter shrugged. "We don't know. We were just told that it had crashed."

Ian broke off the conversation and ran back to the information desk. "Look," he said to the woman, "I've just heard that the Lufthansa plane has crashed. Do you know anything about it? Is anyone hurt? How bad is it?"

The woman shook her head. "I don't know. Phone Lufthansa. I don't know anything."

Ian turned in desperation to a second woman, who was operating a switchboard behind the desk. "Please," he said, "can you get us a line to Lufthansa? We've tried the public phones, but we can't get through."

"All right," she agreed, "I'll try."

They waited, tension and anxiety reflected in their faces, as the woman dialled out, heard an engaged signal, and dialled again. As they stood there, the Horsfields became aware for the first time of the huddles of crying people on the concourse, the groups of reporters, and the cameras. They had walked right through it all without noticing. And they knew then, with a dreadful certainty, that the unthinkable had happened. Something horrific had happened to Flight LH540 . . . and their relatives were aboard.

The switchboard operator looked up. "I've been trying over and over, but the lines are blocked."

"What do we do now?" Ian looked at Patricia in a daze. Nothing prepared you for the absolute horror of a situation like this. What could they do? Then he thought of his younger brother, Robert, working for the Anglo-American Corporation in the centre of Johannesburg. "Bobby," he said to Patricia. "We'll phone Bobby. It'll take him seven or eight minutes to run down to the Lufthansa office. We can meet him there."

Patricia nodded, unable to speak.

"You go and get some money for the phone while I try to get through to Bob."

Patricia took Timothy by the hand and ran to the

bank off the concourse. There were long lines of people waiting at each teller's window. Frustrated by the slowness of everything, she felt like screaming, "Get out of my way! Get out of my way!"

It took her ten minutes to reach a teller. All she wanted was some small change, but the teller seemed to be working in slow motion. Screaming inwardly, Patricia could only watch. Eventually, the coins spilled onto the counter in front of her. She scooped them up and ran back to the public telephones. A tall, blond man dashed past and snatched up a telephone. She saw tears in his eyes and sensed his desperation as he dialled, and dialled, and dialled.

She handed Ian a fistful of coins. He had the telephone pressed to his ear and she could tell by looking at his face that, at that moment, his brother had answered the call.

"Look, Bob," Patricia heard him say, "take it easy now, but Lynn and Earl were supposed to be coming in on that Lufthansa flight this morning, and we think it's crashed."

At the other end of the line in the centre of Johannesburg, Robert Horsfield stood shocked. "Good God," he said hoarsely, thinking of his sister and her children and husband. Gone? He felt ill in his stomach.

"Bob," he heard Ian saying, "we're still out here at

the airport, but they can't tell us anything. And we can't get through to Lufthansa. Their lines are jammed."

Robert Horsfield swallowed, listening.

"Can you get down to their office and see what you can find out? We'll drive in right away and meet you there."

"All right," Robert said, and put down the phone. He felt dazed and shaky, and looked round at the staring faces in his office. His colleagues noticed that the colour had drained from his face.

"I've got to take an hour off," he said quietly. "My sister and her kids were in that jumbo that crashed."

The office fell silent. Everyone looked at Robert. The morning newspapers had headlined the crash across their front pages and there had been reports on the radio. It was the world's first 747 jumbo jet crash, and the initial reports were awful. The aircraft had crashed in flames after take-off from Nairobi Airport and, as far as anyone knew, there were no survivors. But Robert, who had not seen a newspaper that morning, or heard the radio news, knew nothing about it. He had been in bed when the jumbo came crashing down. After a moment's hesitation, he turned and dashed down the stairs, taking them two, three, four at a time.

He left the Anglo-American building and began running along the street. After a block, he slowed to a quick walk. His heart was thumping in his chest, and his suit was sticking to him in the early morning heat as he hurried along the pavement. He shouldered his way between pedestrians, crossed against traffic lights, and intermittently held his breath as he dashed blindly through diesel fumes and smoke. He was trapped in a tunnel of horror. He had visions of his sister. He saw crashing jets in his mind. And he pictured the smiling faces of those two children.

"Why?" he asked himself. "Why?" He remembered the last time he had seen them, three months ago, waiting at the airport in Johannesburg for their overnight flight to Europe. They had farewell drinks up in the lounge overlooking the runways. Through the glass of the window they had looked down on the huge aircraft shining in the floodlight, and there had been laughter and jokes and tears, because they had always been like that, a close and emotional family, the men and the women. None of them could say hello or goodbye without a sudden showing of tears, but that night there had been more than tears. Patricia had said, "I've got a feeling you won't be coming back, just a feeling that we won't see you again."

Lynn had laughed lightly and said, "Oh, you will. You know us, we're always coming and going."

Robert had not thought about it too much at the time, but now the words came back to him and hung heavily in his mind. Patricia had known all along: she had had a feeling, a presentiment, and now it had happened.

Robert pushed through the door of the Lufthansa office and told the women behind the desk, "I've come about the crash. I've got family on board."

They sent him to an office upstairs. A man came through and spoke to him quietly.

"We've just heard from Nairobi. There are maybe fifty survivors. I'm sorry, we have no names. If you can leave your name and telephone number . . . "

Robert walked back to the street. He felt a sudden despair. Only fifty. My God, what were the chances of even one of them surviving? What were the chances? Maybe one of them. There had to be one out of four. There just had to be. But which one? What if one of those boys had survived and was alone right now up there in Nairobi?

He stood on the pavement, staring desolately at the passing traffic, eyes burning, his throat tight. He swallowed hard. That survivor, if there was one, would need help.

Robert turned about and pushed back into the airline office. "I want to book a flight to Nairobi," he said thickly. "I want to go tonight."

For Patricia and Ian Horsfield, the journey back to Johannesburg from the airport was hellish. Patricia had never seen her husband so distraught. His face was white, the tension distorting his mouth and jaw, and he was shaking his head as he drove, saying, "Oh my God, the kids, the kids . . . "

Three-year-old Timothy was protesting, "But I didn't see the plane land! Where's Garett and Brendon?"

Patricia, staring out at the road, shook her head. "I don't know why, but I've got a feeling they're all right. I've just got a feeling."

"But what if Lynn and Earl are unconscious and the boys . . . maybe they've got no legs or something!"

"They're all right," Patricia insisted. "I know they're all right."

But Ian was shaking his head, hands clenching the wheel, and thinking, I can't believe this is happening, it can't be real. I must be dreaming. Any moment now I'll wake up. He reached out his hand like he had read in books and pinched himself, hard, and felt it stinging and knew all of it was real.

"Oh my God," he said. "If a plane like that comes down . . . my God, if they survived, they can't be in once piece."

The countryside, buildings, factories were slipping by. But everything seemed to be happening in slow motion. It felt as if they would never get there. He watched the needle crawling up on the speedometer.

"Don't speed," Patricia told him. "It's not worth it. If we get stopped now . . . "

Yes, Ian thought grimly, I'd probably punch the

bloody traffic cop. I haven't got the time or the patience to argue with anybody right now.

"Those kids," he whispered, and images he had seen of other air crashes passed through his mind. "My God, maybe they're burned."

Then the Horsfields were in the city. They found the Lufthansa office, parked in a no-parking zone — I don't care a damn, Ian thought — and they ran inside. It was the wrong office. They were told to go to another office around the corner, and go up to the fifth floor.

They ran out. A reporter stepped in front of them. "Excuse me . . . "

They brushed him aside, ran to the correct building, rode up in the lift and walked out into the Lufthansa administration offices. A woman in uniform looked at them. She was crying, her eyes red.

"We've come about the Lufthansa flight," Patricia said.

"Who have you got on board?" The woman wiped her nose.

"My sister, her husband and two nephews," Ian said.

"Please come through." She led them to the next office. "He won't be a minute."

They sat and waited. The minutes ticked by. A uniformed man came through with a telex sheet in his hand.

"Will you please give me the name of your relatives."

"Moorhouse," the Horsfields said together.

The man looked down his list. They saw his eyes moving. He looked further down. It seemed such a small piece of paper. Fifty names, that was all. Then his eyes stopped. He began to smile.

"Moorhouse," he read quietly, "G, B, E and L."

Patricia and Ian took Timothy by the hand and caught the lift back to the street. Out on the pavement they saw Robert Horsfield walking towards them, his face taut with worry. Patricia rushed up to him and threw her arms around him, crying, "They're alive! We've just heard they're alive!"

And then, quite suddenly, everyone was crying.

2 • *Flight LH540*

Tuesday, November 19 was a cloudy day in the German city of Frankfurt. Speeding in on the express train carrying us from the World Food Conference in Rome, I looked up at the low-lying clouds and thought, oh no, you're going to fly through that; you and Lynn and the two boys are going to fly through that. And I felt worried.

Then I thought, that's nonsense. You always feel like that on the day you fly, and you always make it. I tried to put the thought out of my mind and considered, instead, the fascinating new life that lay ahead of us.

We were on our way to live in Nairobi, Kenya. There, I would work with the staff of the United Nations Environment Programme as a liaison officer for the Friends of the Earth organisation, which had groups in different parts of the world. Because it was a new post, a few guidelines had been drawn up, but the details had been left to me.

Once we arrived, I would have to set up an office

and a communications network, and begin the long, gradual process of getting to know the various key UN officials. It was an exciting prospect, and Lynn and I had already had a foretaste of what our new life would be like during the three months we spent travelling across Europe. We had financed the trip ourselves so we could meet the people and organisations for whom I would be working.

While we were in Rome, we had queried local airline staff about the possibility of changing our excursion tickets so we could get off the flight in Nairobi, rather than end our trip back in Johannesburg, where we had started. It seemed pointless to go all that way south, and then take another flight back to Nairobi, when the Lufthansa flight would take us through Nairobi anyway.

If the airline agreed, we would get off there and save ourselves all the extra travelling, as well as two take-offs and landings, always the worst part of flying.

But our attempt failed. We were advised to check again with airline officials in Frankfurt, because they might have more flexibility in adjusting the tickets.

So that Tuesday morning, shortly after the express train drew in at Frankfurt, we tried again . . . and failed again. An airline official explained that we could get off the aircraft, but our luggage would be routed according to our tickets and would go on to Johannesburg. What would we do in Nairobi without luggage?

We shrugged, irritated by the inflexibility of the system, and stepped out of the office into the cold grey streets of Frankfurt.

Lynn took my hand as I walked, collar up, into the wind. "*You* could always get off," she said. "They can't really stop you. I'll fly on with the boys and the luggage, and spend a week with Patricia and Ian in Johannesburg while you fix up everything in Nairobi. Then we'll fly up to join you."

I thought about it. It was good idea, but I wasn't sure. "Do you really want to?"

"I'd rather be with you," she said. "But it would save us some money and you'd save a few nerves."

"What about *your* nerves? No," I decided, shaking my head as we turned towards the railway station, "we're all going together."

Occasionally, looking back, I feel ill thinking about what might have happened if we had decided differently.

I made two calls from the international switchboard at the railway station. One was to Lynn's brother, Ian Horsfield, in Johannesburg, to ask him to meet us at the airport in the morning. He laughed, far away down the line in South Africa, and said, "Don't worry about it. I'll take the day off."

The second call was to our author-animal

conservationist friends, Jock and Betty Leslie-Melville, in Nairobi, to tell them we would be flying south through Nairobi in the morning, but we would be back a week later. They were short calls, because talking was expensive, but I felt good when I put down the telephone. In a few hours we would be with the Horsfields. I could see it already: blue skies, the boys splashing about in the pool, while the rest of us relaxed in the sun . . . tomorrow!

"Come on," I picked up the luggage. "Let's get to that airport."

The train from Frankfurt to the airport roared into a tunnel and we were in darkness. The noise beat back off the wall, diminishing as the train slowed. There was a flash of light, and we all blinked. We had arrived at the airport station.

We climbed down off the train, loaded the luggage onto a trolley and pushed it between the people towards the escalator. The trolley had a special fitting underneath, so it could hook onto the moving staircase, and the boys laughed as it caught and climbed the stairs with us.

At the top, the concourse opened up wide, bright and modern. We had been there before, so it was no longer a puzzle. Across the smooth floor we went, rolling the trolley ahead of us to the Lufthansa check-in desk.

I handed over the tickets and the ground stewardess stamped them: first the ticket of my wife, Lynn, then mine, then those of our sons, Garett Jon, who was seven years old, and Brendon Scott, aged six.

"Where would you like to sit?" the stewardess asked. I looked at Lynn.

"In the non-smoking section," she said.

The woman behind the desk smiled and handed over our boarding passes. She had seated us in row 26, between the wings on the port side of the Boeing 747: Brendon next to the window, Garett in the centre seat, then me, with the aisle on my right. Lynn would be sitting in the first seat across the aisle.

The boys pushed the trolley to the baggage check. I picked up the cases and placed them on the scale. On the trolley stood my portable typewriter in its dark maroon travelling case. I picked it up.

"Will it be all right with the luggage," I asked the stewardess, "or should I take it with me?"

She nodded, laughing, "It will be quite safe with the other things."

I placed it on the scale and patted it. Another trip for you, old friend. Hands came up and lifted all of our luggage onto a conveyor belt.

I never saw the typewriter again.

Lufthansa's Flight LH275 from Milan had just landed and the jet nosed in next to the terminal, engines shrieking. Marketing co-ordinator Malcolm Solts, aged thirty-four, from Boston, Massachusetts, picked up his hand luggage and stepped off.

A few minutes later he was walking down a long airport corridor to the check-in desk. He had been travelling for weeks, it seemed, making great leaps across the globe. First, a flight across the Atlantic to Britain, then a short hop over to France, then on to Spain, next Italy, and up to Germany to catch the long flight to South Africa. It had been business all the way, and meeting after meeting with members of the far-flung Gillette company. Different accents, different boardrooms. Thousands of miles in a few days, but he didn't think too much about it. For him, it was almost a way of life.

The ground stewardess handed him his boarding pass, red for first class, and he tucked it safely away and headed for one of the business lounges. It was shortly after four in the afternoon and he had nearly five and a half hours before the flight left for Johannesburg.

Malcolm Solts got himself a drink from the bar, made himself comfortable in one of the chairs and spread out his papers. The lounge was a good, quiet place. He relaxed for a moment, sipping at his drink, then took out his pen and began working on his reports.

Herman Hennecke spent the evening wandering

about the shops on the concourse at Frankfurt Airport. Christmas was still five weeks away, but there were gifts on sale that would be impossible to find in Johannesburg, and he knew his sons, Ulf, who was ten, and seven-year-old Ralf, were expecting "something special" from the toy shops of Europe. He smiled, thinking about them and his wife, half a world away, and guessed they would be excited when they saw what he had in his packages.

He had been away for nearly two weeks, attending the budget talks of the Olympia Business Machines company, at Wilhelmshaven, on the German North Sea coast, in his capacity as managing director of the South African company. After the talks were over, he spent the weekend with his parents at Bodenwerder, in the Weser valley, near Hannover, and now he was on his way home.

The thought of flying did not bother him. He already had one flight behind him that Tuesday evening. Barely an hour before, he had touched down aboard Lufthansa's Flight LH725 from Hannover.

Herman Hennecke picked up his parcels and few items of luggage and walked across the concourse to the Lufthansa check-in desk. He presented his ticket.

"Where would you like to sit?" the ground stewardess asked him.

"Somewhere in the centre, between the wings," he told her. "It's smoother there. I'd like to get in a little sleep on the long flight, if that's possible."

"Certainly." The stewardess handed him a boarding pass. She had given him seat 4 in row 26.

"Thank you," he smiled. From there, he would be able to see the in-flight movie and, if the aircraft was not too full, he might be able to kick off his shoes and stretch out over three or four seats for a sleep. I'll be fresh when I get to Johannesburg, he thought, and almost in time for lunch.

He picked up his briefcase and headed for the international lounge.

The oldest person taking the flight was eighty-eight-year-old inventor Erich Hesse, who lived part of the year in Berlin and spent the rest of the time at Bremervörde, in northern Germany. He sat in the small departure lounge with his attaché case on his knees, his hands resting on it lightly, as he peered through his glasses at his fellow passengers. He was determined not to let the case out of his sight. In it lay the precious papers that were his life's work, technical designs for wind-powered energy generation, and he did not want to lose them.

Erich Hesse was flying to Johannesburg to celebrate his eighty-ninth birthday on December 26 with his daughter, Gisela Hutton, his son-in-law and his three young grandchildren. They were due to meet him at the airport in the morning and drive him to their suburban home in Linksfield, north-east of the Johannesburg city centre. Until he reached their house, he intended keeping his case as close to him as possible. Losing his papers at this point in his life would be an absolute disaster.

Also waiting at the airport for the departure of Flight LH540 was forty-four-year-old Marie Galitzine, of Paris, who was making her first trip to Africa as a Unitours travel company guide. A last-minute change of plans had put her in charge of a party of twelve Americans. The guide scheduled for the trip had withdrawn, and Marie had been asked to fill the gap, despite the fact that she had not been to Africa before. Until now, she had conducted tours only around Europe.

Taking over the tour had forced her to cancel her own two-week holiday on the Riviera, but she did not mind. She was fascinated by Africa and here, at last, she was within hours of seeing it.

Marie met the Americans for the first time in Frankfurt, a few hours before the flight was due to take off. They were a mixed group of four married couples and four single women, who had flown from the United States to Amsterdam, and travelled on from there to Frankfurt.

The oldest members were Alfred and Veronica Solibakke, both seventy-seven, of Seattle, Washington, close to where Boeing 747 aircraft were built. The youngest in the party was Nancy Kahn, who had recently turned seventeen, and was travelling with her parents Karl and Renate Kahn, of Dallas, Texas. There were two more from Dallas: Tillie Harmel and her sister, Gladys Golman.

The other group members were Edmund and Elinor Senkler, of Seattle, Elbert and Peggy Ottenheimer, of Baltimore, and Salome Zeiss, from Pasadena, California.

The group had spent the day sightseeing in Frankfurt and arrived at the airport at about eight in the evening. Marie Galitzine was anxious to get them all checked in and their luggage weighed early, so she urged them along to the Lufthansa desk, Karl Kahn helping the Solibakkes to load up their trolley and wheeling it along for them with the rest of the party. By now, the atmosphere between the members of the group was relaxed. Already, they were like old friends, laughing and chatting, and excited by the prospect of seeing Africa in the morning.

Marie Galitzine slid herself up onto the baggage counter and sat swinging her feet. She invited them to choose their seats. They were all travelling on economy tickets, but there were different places they could sit. Up front, behind the first class section in the nose, was the quiet compartment, where there would be no movie. Behind that, between the wings, was the section for non-smokers and those who wanted to see the movie. And finally, stretching from row 32, about halfway down the long aircraft fuselage to the tail, was the smoking section, where passengers could also see the movie.

Marie Galitzine was a smoker. Because of this, she told her tour group, she would be sitting in the back of the aircraft. The twelve Americans, including teenager Nancy Kahn, who was another smoker, chose to sit in the non-smoking section between the wings. This meant Nancy would have to stroll to the rear of the aircraft each time she felt the urge to light up a cigarette. But, despite the inconvenience, she preferred to be near her parents and the rest of the group.

Their check-in complete, the members of the tour group wandered about the airport, gazing idly at items in the shops and display cabinets. Karl Kahn, feeling that the Solibakkes probably needed a helping hand, picked up their hand luggage and dropped it back on their trolley so they could wheel it about. After that there was nothing more that needed doing. The Unitours travellers whiled away the remaining time.

Travel agent John Bing and his wife Jean, who lived in Johannesburg, arrived at Frankfurt Airport loaded with Turkish souvenirs.

We look like Christmas trees with all our parcels,

John Bing thought as they walked through the airport building. They had collected most of their presents in Istanbul while attending the annual conference of the Universal Federation of Travel Agents' Associations. The meeting had been a memorable one for the Bings. John, already president of the South African Association of Travel Agents, had been elected chairman of the international body's African region. The election made him eligible for service on the board of directors.

On their return journey, the Bings stayed briefly in Frankfurt as guests of the German National Tourist Office, and collected some computerised accounts from the German Travel Agents' Association. It had been a highly successful trip.

Then, at the check-in desk, the Bings discovered they had been booked forward of the wings. They did not like this position. Having flown thousands of miles across the world in Boeing 747s, they knew the flight would be smoothest over the wings. They asked if they could change their seats.

"Certainly," the ground stewardess said. She examined her seating plan. "Where would you prefer?"

They pointed to the middle-wing area.

The stewardess wrote out their boarding passes. She had moved them to row 31, the last of the seats in the non-smoking section between the wings, with the toilet cabinets close behind. The Bings gathered their parcels together, hoping for a half-empty flight so they could stretch out and sleep on the overnight leg to Nairobi.

We had time to kill. I took my son Brendon for a walk to see the shops in the international lounge. A group of nuns passed by and smiled at him.

We walked on past a chapel. Through the door I saw people praying.

"What's that?" Brendon asked.

"A church."

"A church at the airport?"

"Yes," I said.

"What for?"

"People like to pray before they fly. You can see some of the people in there now."

"Yes," he said, looking, "I can see three. What do they pray for?"

"For a safe journey, for God to look after the friends they're leaving behind. All sorts of things."

"Can we pray too?"

"If you like. Do you want to?"

"No," Brendon said. "Let's go back to Mama."

We walked back and Lynn said, "Where have you been? They're calling our flight."

"I'm sorry. We were looking at the shops."

I picked up the hand luggage and we walked in a group up the long corridor that led to our flight's departure lounge.

In the small lounge Hermann Hennecke toyed with his glasses as he waited for boarding to begin. He heard laughter, turned and saw a group of American tourists joking with each other. They were dressed casually, cameras and hand luggage slung over their shoulders, and looked as if they were going on safari. Lucky people.

Hermann glanced at the others sitting around him: a group of nuns, couples with children, people spending the last few minutes reading the day's newspapers. His eyes travelled on, noticing the time on the digital clock. The figures were clicking steadily towards 21.00 hours, and he thought, We'll be lucky if we get away on time. Beyond the windows, Lufthansa's Boeing 747 *Hessen* glinted in the floodlights.

Bob Laburn, fifty-four, was one of the last to arrive at the lounge. The chief engineer of the Rand Water Board in Johannesburg looked through the doorway, saw the full seats and groups of passengers milling about and decided to wait out in the passage. He turned back and sat on a bench next to a couple with a young child. They were smiling and talking quietly.

Bob Laburn was fiddling with his boarding pass as he waited, and his thoughts went back to the last few days he had spent in Europe. He had been to a conference of the International Water Suppliers Association in Berlin. The association's scientific and technical council met every two years and he was chairman of one of the committees. It had been a short, hard-working trip with little time for relaxation, and he felt tired and pleased to be heading home. It was all over for another two years.

He glanced at the seat number on his pass. Row 1. He would be sitting right up front, in the first class section, with a window at his right elbow. He always liked a window seat and always asked for one. Getting the first row, right up in the nose, was the luck of the draw.

Hans Neeb, from Minden, near Hannover, sat watching the mothers with their young children, and thought of his own wife and their two young sons. By now they would be getting ready for bed, if they weren't there already. He smiled to himself and wished for a moment that he was back home instead of waiting at an airport to make a journey halfway across the world.

In the last four years he had flown the route four or five times a year to enable him to spend a few weeks at the South African subsidiary of his firm, Eisenwerk Weserhütte, in Johannesburg. He had set up the subsidiary himself; he was one of the directors and liked to have first-hand knowledge of its progress. He often took the night flight from Frankfurt, snatching a few hours of sleep during the journey, and arriving in Johannesburg shortly before lunch.

As he waited, only minutes before take-off, he saw a business associate he knew: Anthony Grant, managing director of Southern Cross Steel, and president of the Pretoria Portland Cement company. The two men shook hands and spoke briefly. There was a good deal they wanted to discuss.

"I'll come and see you after we've taken off," Hans Neeb told the South African.

Mother Superior Dietlinde Geis, who was forty-six, was happy to be nearing the start of her flight. She was on her way back to her mission work at the Holy Childhood Convent, at Eshowe, in Zululand, after spending her home leave with the sisters of her "mother" convent at Würzburg-Oberzell, in northern Bavaria.

While she waited, she met four nuns from the Solanus Convent at Landshut, north-east of Munich: Sister Annuntiata Maier, sixty-three, Sister Richardis Setzer, sixty-two, Sister Bona Hämmerle, seventy-two, and Sister Blandina Hohenleitner, fifty-two. They, too, had been on home leave and were now on the return journey to the mission station at Harding, in eastern South Africa, where they had worked for more than thirty years.

Mother Dietlinde did not belong to their order and had not met them before, but they had a lot in common, and they talked pleasantly about their work. They were all a little excited. Tomorrow they would be back with the people they knew, carrying out their tasks in the sunshine and dry African heat.

Finally the nuns parted, wishing each other a pleasant flight and God's blessing for their continuing work. The four Solanus sisters returned to their seats and Mother Dietlinde sat alone. Her thoughts turned to the days she had spent with the sisters of Würzburg-Oberzell. She knew she would think of them all with fondness and perhaps a little sadness in the days ahead. And she would think of Germany, so far away.

Then it was time to board. Mother Dietlinde bowed her head as the people began standing up and prayed, "God, protect this flight." She sat a while in silence, then picked up her bags, went through the final security check and boarded the aircraft.

Hermann Hennecke stepped through the narrow passageway from the departure lounge into *Hessen*, and saw the soft lights, the rows of seats stretching way back towards the tail, and the stewardesses in their yellow jackets moving between the shuffling passengers.

He handed over his boarding pass and a stewardess showed him to his seat.

"Thank you," he nodded.

Hermann packed his parcels away in the overhead locker. He placed his briefcase on the seat next to him, sat down and buckled himself in. The people were still filing in, but it was not so crowded now, and he looked about, feeling pleased with his position. The aisle was one seat away to his right and there were empty seats all around him. The closest passenger was a young woman to his left. Across the far aisle sat what looked like the rest of the family, a man and two young boys.

He looked at his watch. Yes, they were a little late. The hands were edging on for 21.40, but they would probably make up the lost time during the night.

Edmund and Elinor Senkler stepped into the jumbo jet and saw their fellow tourists Alfred and Veronica Solibakke already sitting down, close to the door.

"How did you manage to get such good seats?" Edmund asked as they passed. But the Solibakkes were not happy. They wanted to change their position, they told the Senklers, and later moved further forward.

The Senklers walked on down to their seats on the port side, strapped in and looked out at the lights glinting off the broad surface of the wing directly beneath them.

There was a fresh red rose waiting for each of

Hessen's first class passengers as they were shown forward to their places in the aircraft's nose. The long-stemmed roses were attached to the seats by the stewardesses and were accompanied by the usual first class offerings: a pack of stationery, aircraft slippers for those who wanted to shed their shoes, a menu and a "welcome aboard" cocktail of champagne and orange juice. After take-off there would be more free drinks, cigars and cigarettes, a gourmet dinner, chocolates, cognac and liqueurs.

Bob Laburn settled himself and fastened his seat belt. To his right was the window he had asked for and through it he could see the lights of the airport and the small vehicles moving about the runway. The man in the twinned seat alongside him did not introduce himself and, probably because they spoke different languages, they did not try to talk to each other.

Also in the first class section sat West German Bundestag Vice-President Liselotte Funcke and three other Bundestag members, Dr Curt Becker, Dr Rolf Böhme and Rudolf Müller, who would disembark at Nairobi in the morning to begin an official visit to Kenya.

Globe-trotting Malcolm Solts had an aisle seat four rows from the front, on the left side of the aircraft. At the check-in he had asked for a seat in the non-smoking section, and this was what the stewardess had given him, a seat not far from the staircase that wound up to the first class cocktail lounge.

He sat waiting for the aircraft to move off and looked about him, seeing his fellow passengers for the first time. Closed off in the business lounge from the usual pre-flight crowds, he had worked steadily on his reports throughout the afternoon and into the evening, and then he had taken a walk to the duty-free shops to buy gifts for his family. He had not met any other passengers until he stepped on board, but there was little time for conversation. It was almost time to go.

Outside, the engines began howling and, looking down, I saw workmen moving about in the half-light. The sound of the engines changed and the airport building appeared to swing away. The big jet was taxiing.

At the head of the runway the engines built to a roar, the jet bobbed a little and then, whoosh, we were off, hurtling down the runway. I looked left and saw the lights going flash-flash by. The buildings were blurring past. Faster, faster, I said in my mind, and a strange daredevil feeling took over. We could all go up in flames if something went wrong, yet here I was gambling with life, exhilarated by the surging power, the race towards oblivion, or take-off. Come on, get there, my mind shouted. Get there! The lights were streaming past, the nose lifted, there was a jerk, air under the wheels, and then we were off, screaming up slowly against gravity.

Thrust back against the seat, I willed the aircraft on. The critical moment passed, and we rose into the night sky with the lights of Germany falling away steadily below us.

I looked across the aisle at Lynn. She looked at me, sighed and smiled.

It was time for cocktails. Hermann Hennecke sat nursing a Bloody Mary and began reading the paperback detective novel he had bought at Frankfurt Airport. He did not have long to read. Soon, there was a rattling of trays, and the cabin staff came down the aisle with the heated-up dinners and placed one on his folded-down seat-tray. Hermann smoothed out his paper napkin and began to eat.

It was a smooth and pleasant flight. There was almost no turbulence, only the steady pulsing of the engines. Hermann ate on, feeling relaxed. He was looking forward to the Clint Eastwood movie to while away an hour or so. *Dead End* was an odd title, but he guessed it would be lively enough. Eastwood movies usually were.

He looked to his left and smiled at the young woman sitting a seat away. She was nibbling at a dry biscuit, and a cup of tea stood next to the small packet on the tray in front of her.

"I can't eat anything when I'm flying," Lynn told him.

Hermann nodded. "Are those your two boys over there?"

She looked across the aisle at her husband and two young boys tucking into the big dinner. "Yes," she nodded. "Garett and Brendon."

"They must be about the same age as my two boys. They even look like them."

"Oh, they all look alike at this age. I don't know why." She smiled and bit into her biscuit.

They lapsed into silence and did not speak again until it was all over.

At row 38, towards the rear of the aircraft, Hans Neeb and Anthony Grant held their promised in-flight business discussion. They were deeply involved in their conversation and did not pay any attention to the antics of the young children in the next aisle, to the nuns, or to any of their fellow passengers.

The arrival of dinner brought them back to their surroundings. A stewardess was handing out the trays. Hans Neeb stood up in the aisle, feeling he would have liked to have spoken a bit longer to his business friend.

"Perhaps we can continue our discussion tomorrow morning between Nairobi and Johannesburg," he suggested, and Anthony Grant agreed.

Hans Neeb edged past the stewardesses, smiled a greeting at John Hall, general manager of Southern Cross Steel, who was sitting a row ahead of Anthony Grant, and returned to his seat. He had a fairly long walk. His seat was located in the economy class quiet compartment, directly behind the first class section.

The dinner trays were stacked away and, in the dim after-dinner light, many passengers prepared to watch Clint Eastwood on the screen, hearing the soundtrack through plastic earphones. Others decided to ignore the movie and listen instead to six channels of pre-recorded music. Some read, angling the small ceiling lamps so the light pooled on the printed page. And a handful simply dozed fitfully, while the jet rumbled on through the night.

Malcolm Solts, sitting in the first class section, did not feel like watching the movie. He had spent the early part of the flight reading and then chatting to the German couple from Düsseldorf, who were seated behind him. The man, he guessed, was about fifty and had told him they were going to South Africa to visit friends and spend some time in the sun. It had been pleasant talking to them, swapping stories, smiling a bit, and whiling away the time before dinner, and now that dinner was over, he didn't feel like staring at Clint Eastwood.

Solts got up, stretched his legs, and climbed the

stairs to the cocktail lounge on the upper deck. It was perhaps the closest that aircraft had come to matching the luxury of the great ocean liners: a private lounge high up in the star-filled sky.

He got himself a drink, sat down in an upholstered chair and chatted to a woman sitting nearby. She told him she was originally from England, but was now living in Germany and working for an accounting firm. Tonight she was on her way to Johannesburg for a business meeting.

They talked on. Beyond the portholes of the lounge the stars shifted slowly in the dark. And down in the cabin below Clint Eastwood smiled grimly, chasing after his busload of hijacked children.

Much later someone came up the stairs. Malcolm Solts looked up and saw it was the German who had been sitting in the seat behind him.

"May I join you?" the German asked.

"Certainly."

The newcomer got himself a drink and came over, and they sat, talking and drinking, two strangers drawing closer and closer to Nairobi with each sweeping second.

In the economy class section, Unitours party member Renate Kahn was restless and unable to sleep, so she wandered along to the rear of the aircraft and sat talking to the tour guide, Marie Galitzine.

The conversation confirmed Renate's opinion that Marie was a charming and delightful person, who would certainly help to make their African tour a great success. Marie seemed to make friends easily and already had all her tour group members calling her "Maya". Several of them, including fellow-smoker Nancy Kahn, had strolled back to pass the time with her, sharing a drink, chatting, or in Nancy's case, by having a smoke.

While she was in the tail section, Renate Kahn also met the children's stewardess, Helge Nachtsheim, who was entertaining a group of about six youngsters while their parents watched the movie. Helge was known as a "Mickey Mouse", because of the large, smiling Disney character that appeared on the front of her uniform. Lufthansa's route to South Africa was the only one that offered this service. To become a "Mickey Mouse", Helge told Renate, you had to be able to speak German and English, and you had to be a mother. Helge satisfied both requirements. Back home in Johannesburg she had sons of two and eleven, who were being looked after by a relative.

She had been kept busy on this flight, reading and playing games with the children, and she had a hunch she would be busy right through the night. But she did not mind. She enjoyed looking after children, and they seemed to like being with her.

This flight was different from other flights she had

made on this route, Helge said, and smiled towards the man sitting at the back of the aircraft . . . her husband, Klaus. He had been on a business trip to Germany and had hired Elke Stosch, a thirty-year-old interpreter from Düsseldorf, as a secretary for his firm in Johannesburg. They had worked together in Germany several years ago, before the Nachtsheims emigrated to South Africa.

Klaus had arranged his trip so they could all be on the same flight, and had managed to get two seats next to Helge's, so they could sit together. But the "Mickey Mouse" did not use her seat for much more than take-offs and landings. She was too busy. Most of the time, she told Renate Kahn, she was on her feet, attending to the children.

Clint Eastwood had chased the kidnapper to a bloody death. The screens faded as the movie ended, and now there was only music, or sleep. But Renate Kahn was still restless, and wandered about the aircraft.

Earlier, after take-off from Frankfurt, she had toured the cabin, looking for two or three unoccupied seats in a row where her daughter Nancy could stretch out for the night. Eventually, in the rear section, she found two alongside the group of nuns, and placed coats on them to show that they had been taken.

But Nancy was not interested in sleeping that night,

and after a while she suggested to her mother, "Why don't you go and take the coats and things off those seats, so someone else can have them?"

"Are you sure?"

"I really don't feel like sleeping," Nancy told her.

Renate turned back to remove the coats and noticed a nun sitting many rows away from the others, in a completely different part of the aircraft. Perhaps she would like to take over those seats, Renate thought.

She went up to the nun and said to her in German, "Your sisters are sitting in the back and I've found some empty places right next to them. Wouldn't you prefer to be with them? You might enjoy sitting there and stretching out for the night. There's plenty of space."

The nun smiled and thanked her. Yes, she would like to be with the others. She got up, reached for her bag and walked with Renate to the seats still draped with the coats, alongside her fellow sisters.

Renate removed the coats and the nun sat down and made herself comfortable, smiling at Renate.

"Thank you very much," she said. "You are very kind."

Well, Renate thought, heading back to the seats where her husband Karl lay dozing, at least I've made someone happy. I hope she can manage to sleep.

It was quiet in the aircraft. The lights were dimmed

and the plastic slides had been drawn down over the windows. *Hessen* had flown high over the Alps, crossed southern Europe and the darkened Mediterranean, and thrust on now through the sky like an arrow above the vast sleeping African plains.

Hermann Hennecke kicked off his shoes and stretched out on the empty seats. He placed a pillow under his head and drew the blanket up under his chin. For a while he listened to the hissing of the air conditioning, and felt the gentle bobbing as the jet powered ahead, and then he fell asleep.

3 • *An African departure*

It was raining in Nairobi. The drops fell in long lines past the neon lights shining from the hotel rooftops, splashed heavily into the night-darkened streets and swirled away down the gutters and drains. Beyond the city, in the open fields and bush, rain turned the earth into a thick mud that clung to boots and shoes and feet and wheels.

In a room at the Intercontinental Hotel, not far from the towering Kenyatta Conference Centre in the heart of the city, nine Lufthansa cabin crew members sat talking and joking and laughing. Their three-day rest period was drawing to a close and they had been invited to spend the last few hours before bed in the room of Captain Norbert Diekmann, a twenty-three-year-old German Federal Border Guard, who had been seconded to Nairobi as a security officer.

He got on well with the flying crews, and enjoyed driving them around the city, showing them the sights, fetching and carrying. But he thought this particular crew was even better than usual . . . a truly lively crowd. They had arrived in Nairobi in the early hours of Sunday morning aboard a 747 from Frankfurt and looked extremely tired. Surprisingly, after a few hours of sleep, they soon recovered and by the next afternoon were already planning an all-night party.

The party, held on Monday night at the home of a German businessman friend, was a great success. The talking, dancing and drinking went on until the early hours and ended only when the stewards and stewardesses straggled back to their rooms at the Intercontinental. One or two of them even managed a nightcap up in Norbert Diekmann's room.

But on their final night, because they were due to take off for Johannesburg shortly before eight in the morning, there was no drinking. Lufthansa regulations prohibited any crew member from drinking alcohol twelve hours before a flight.

Instead, the crew members relaxed on the hotel furniture, talking among themselves. They would still have another two rest days in Nairobi when they got back from Johannesburg aboard Wednesday night's northbound flight. They were all looking forward to it . . . another two days in Nairobi and, with luck, the sun would be shining all the time.

In a different room at the Intercontinental, the fifty-three-year-old crew commander for the next morning's flight, Captain Christian Krack, was getting ready for an early night's sleep. He had returned that afternoon from a wildlife safari in a rented Volkswagen with his wife Erika and his daughter Karin.

They had flown out from Germany on the Saturday flight, slept off the initial effects at the hotel on the Sunday morning, and then driven north-west, taking the road that runs along the floor of the Rift Valley to Lake Naivasha. There, they had spent Sunday night, and travelled on the next morning, heading in a south-westerly direction to the Keekorok Lodge in the Masai Mara Reserve.

The next day they drove for hours across the African plains, searching out the lions, elephants, rhinos and herds of buffaloes that migrated northwards across the Tanzanian border from Serengeti. Tired after their enthralling day, the Kracks slept overnight at the lodge and travelled back to Nairobi the next afternoon.

The three-day safari had been a relaxed and happy time for the Kracks, and especially for Karin. The trip to Africa was a birthday gift from her father. In the morning, Wednesday, November 20, she would be twenty-two. And while her father flew the incoming Boeing 747 south to Johannesburg, she and her mother planned to go bargain-hunting in the shops of Nairobi.

Fifty-year-old Flight Engineer Rudi Hahn was

already in bed and drifting off to sleep. He had spent his three-day rest period working on his income tax declaration in his hotel room, and the hours of paperwork had tired him out. He had few, if any, concerns about the next morning's flight. In his career, he had already notched up 13,236 flying hours, 2,650 of them on Boeing 747 jumbo jets, and felt quite relaxed about it all. He had been flying for Lufthansa since 1955, first on Lockheeds and then on Boeing 707s and 727s, and was finally checked out for duty on 747s in March 1971.

The flight engineer was in good physical shape and in good health. He had sailed through his last medical check just over four months ago. His licence was endorsed "Holder to carry reading glasses," but in reality he needed to use them only when his eyes were tired or when the light was poor. That did not happen often, and rarely in Africa.

The on-off rain had kept the co-pilot, First Officer Hans-Joachim Schacke, in the hotel for most of the three-day break. But he was not particularly interested in rushing about "having fun". He had been to Nairobi twelve times already and felt he had seen all the sights and done almost all the things he could do in the city.

Schacke was thirty-five and had flown Starfighters for the West German Air Force before joining Lufthansa in 1968. The airline started him as a co-pilot on Boeing 727s and switched him to Boeing 747s in 1971 after he had undergone conversion training. Since then, he had clocked up 2,237 hours as a 747 co-pilot. Only a few of those hours had been in the company of Captain Krack. The first time had been a week ago, when they flew a Lufthansa 747 freighter between Frankfurt and New York.

The next morning's take-off would be his thirteenth from Nairobi Airport, out on the fields beyond the city. The co-pilot switched off the bedroom lights and tried to sleep.

At 5.15 that Wednesday morning, November 20, while a gloomy semi-darkness still covered the city of Nairobi, the seven men and ten women who made up the relief crew for *Hessen* were woken from their sleep. In their different rooms at the Intercontinental Hotel they took out their uniforms and began dressing: dark navy blue uniforms for the men, and bright yellow summer outfits for the women. When they had dressed, they packed a few items they would need for their short stay in the "golden city" of Johannesburg.

Captain Krack went through and wished his daughter a happy birthday, said goodbye to his wife and went down to the hotel lobby to meet his crew. Co-pilot Schacke arrived and Krack saw Flight Engineer Hahn coming across the lobby to join them. Both Schacke and Hahn appeared relaxed and rested, although Schacke felt he hadn't slept too well. They stood quietly together, the three men who, in a few minutes, would be at the controls of *Hessen*. The cabin crew began assembling while the captain stared through the glass front of the hotel, watching for the two Volkswagen minibuses that would take them all to the airport.

The buses appeared suddenly in the half-light, making a quick turn into the hotel forecourt, and drew up outside the entrance. The cockpit crew picked up their hand luggage and walked out, and behind them straggled the cabin crew. Some of the crew were late and came running up behind the rest. Purser Heidi Tischer scolded them, and after some light-hearted banter they were all seated in the buses.

The engines revved and the leading bus nosed out of the hotel grounds onto the road, with the second bus close behind. They turned once more and accelerated down the Uhuru Highway, past the Kenyan Parliament Buildings, climbed the hump over the railway line, and motored smoothly along the Mombasa road in the direction of the airport.

The light was improving all the time, the early morning mist slowly dispersing and the sombre sky brightening. The buses drove on steadily, the wheels splashing through puddles on the still-wet road. A sign pointed to the airport. They swung off left and far ahead the crew saw the terminal building.

The minibuses drew up at the terminal entrance and the crew of seventeen picked up their bags and strolled into the building. They walked across the concourse and headed off down a passageway to the room where they would have their final pre-flight briefing.

Many miles away, high above the misty bush, *Hessen* was gradually losing altitude as it made its approach.

Back in the centre of Nairobi, a third minibus toured the streets, calling at hotels to take passengers to the airport. Waiting impatiently for its arrival was Margaret Hooker, who was booked to join the Lufthansa flight leaving that morning for Johannesburg. She had spent the night in a hotel in the Kenyan capital after flying in from Jeddah, Saudi Arabia, and stood with her baggage close beside her, staring out at the road.

She let out a sigh of relief when she saw the minibus emerge from the early morning mist. Before it had even stopped she was hurrying out to board it. She was anxious to be on her way, because she was racing against time. Her mother, seventy-seven-year-old Maggie Laing, was lying seriously ill in Cape Town, South Africa, and family members were worried that she might not survive to celebrate her seventy-eighth birthday on December 3.

The day before, Margaret had said goodbye to her civil engineer husband David in Jeddah and boarded a Pakistani Airlines flight to Nairobi. From there, this morning's Lufthansa flight would take her as far as Johannesburg, where she would be met by her brother, break her journey briefly, and then fly on to her mother's bedside in Cape Town.

Margaret Hooker climbed onto the minibus and was surprised to see that there was only one other passenger. This passenger was a woman about her age and, as the bus continued its journey through the city to the airport, they began talking. Her name was Carol Mall, and she was an American, aged forty-seven, who had been working in Addis Ababa, Ethiopia, for the Agency For International Development, which administered the foreign aid programme of the United States government. Carol told Margaret Hooker she was on holiday, and had decided to visit Cape Town and Johannesburg.

"Johannesburg?"

Carol Mall nodded, and Margaret thought about the city she knew so well, and wondered where Carol would go and what she would do in a place like that. It was such a big, sprawling city, and it could get terribly lonely for a woman on her own.

"Look," she told Carol, "I'm going to be staying for a time with my sister in Germiston. That's almost the same city. You tell me where you are, and I'll phone you, so we can arrange something."

They exchanged numbers and addresses, chatting as the bus drove out across the flat countryside. By the time it drew up outside the airport terminal they were already good friends.

4 • *Fifty minutes to live*

Dawn broke aboard *Hessen* and down below were the yellow-brown fields of Africa. Those passengers who had been sleeping opened their eyes and stretched their stiff limbs.

Elinor Senkler had spent the night on two empty seats in the tail section and got up when she heard the clatter of breakfast trays. The people around her appeared a bit rumpled, and there were blankets and pillows over the seats, and shoes and bags and belongings strewn across the floor. Only the nuns, sitting upright in their dark habits, looked neat and collected, a picture of serenity in the shambles around them.

Looking back, Elinor saw a young mother sitting at the rear of the jumbo with a sleepy child on her lap. Fussing about between her and the other children was "Mickey Mouse" Helge Nachtsheim, still looking cheerful after the long night. The stewardesses came down the aisles, offering a pre-landing snack, but many settled for a simple cup of hot coffee.

Elinor gathered up her belongings and walked back to rejoin her husband Edmund in the economy compartment between the wings. She sat down and buckled herself in for landing.

Minutes later, the seat belt signs came on and there was an announcement about not smoking. The aircraft descended steadily and down below the passengers could see the buildings of Nairobi and ribbons of roadways against the earth. Shortly before seven o' clock, Kenyan time, *Hessen* came skimming in over the bush and touched down gently on the runway at Nairobi Airport. It was a beautiful landing, so smooth and so well judged that the passengers began applauding.

The headlong speed reduced steadily, and the big jet taxied off to the service area, turned, was guided in by ground staff, and stopped. The engines shut off and the vibration that had been there all the way from Frankfurt came to an abrupt end. The mobile steps came rolling up, the exit doors were swung open, and a strange silence seemed to flood in.

With their briefing over, the new crew members stepped out of the airport building onto the tarmac. There, glinting in the soft morning light, stood *Hessen*, the huge jet towering high above the service vehicles, and dwarfing all the other aircraft waiting on the apron.

The cabin crew walked together towards the aircraft, bags slung over their shoulders, some carrying hand luggage. Directly ahead, two sets of mobile steps had been rolled up to the aircraft doors. A catering vehicle came past.

Then, in the pale early morning sun, something happened that lodged in the mind of Tom Scott, a tall, dark-haired American-born steward, aged twenty-four, whose initial three-month probation period with the airline was coming to an end. Four members of the cabin crew with cameras ran on ahead and turned, like tourists, to snap a quick photograph of their approaching friends. There were smiles and grins, followed by a bit of face-pulling as Manfred Vohs, twenty-seven, Rolf Nietser, twenty-eight, Renate Kriegleder, twenty-four, and twenty-two-year-old Rita Selbach snapped away. It was unusual and unexpected, but Tom Scott didn't think too much about it then. Later, the incident would replay itself vividly in his mind over and over again.

Captain Krack and his crew waited at the foot of the forward steps and peered up at the doorway as the disembarking passengers began coming out. On this morning the relief crew members were accompanied by the West German ambassador to Kenya, Dr Harald Heimsoeth. He was at the airport to welcome the four parliamentarians at the start of their official visit.

Down the steps they came, led by the Vice-President, Liselotte Funcke. They shook hands and were escorted away by Dr Heimsoeth. More passengers followed and, finally, the cockpit crew who had flown *Hessen* through the night from Frankfurt. The two captains greeted each other and Captain Krack was told: no defects or difficulties. *Hessen* was in excellent shape.

The relief crew went on board. Captain Krack, First Officer Schacke and Flight Engineer Hahn went forward to the first class compartment and climbed the staircase to the cocktail lounge, entering the cockpit through the connecting door. On the deck below, cabin crew members took up their positions by the doors. This was a standard safety precaution, in case the aircraft caught fire during refuelling and the crew had to evacuate the passengers.

Tom Scott stood by the open door immediately forward of the port wing. Alongside him was Check Purser Jürgen Freund, who was on the flight to assess Tom's performance and that of the other two probationers, Christel Pilz, aged twenty-four, and Monika Spiegl, twenty. All the working positions for the flight had been decided by drawing lots before they left Frankfurt on Saturday night, and they would keep to them throughout the African journey. Tom Scott had drawn a position in the economy section, between the wings, alongside a small kitchen where the in-flight meals were heated. Stationed there, he would share the twin fold-down crew seats in the doorway with Jürgen Freund during the take-off. They would strap in, sitting shoulder-to-shoulder, facing towards the tail, shortly before the roll began.

The four crew members who had snapped photographs of their colleagues on the apron a few minutes before, had all drawn positions in the 747's tail compartment. They had fifty minutes to live.

The Kahn family were up and walking about the aircraft soon after it stopped on the apron. They watched the new crew arriving on board and taking up their positions by the doors, and then teenager Nancy became absorbed in lacing up her hiking boots. These boots were big and comfortable, and she had brought them with her because she felt sure she would be doing a lot of rough walking in Africa. She had kicked them off during the night and walked about the aircraft in her socks but, on landing, had put them back on, thinking she might get off during the refuelling stop.

But the Kahns did not get off. The stop was too short and, seeing that they would be coming back to Nairobi in a few weeks anyway as part of their tour, it did not seem worth the trouble, just to see the airport terminal. All airports looked about the same. Nancy agreed, but decided to leave her boots on.

Her father, Karl Kahn, had spent the night stretched

out on the centre economy section seats and had slept for several hours. He took himself off to the toilets for a wash. He found one empty, went in, washed and even managed to shave before there was a hammering on the door. Surprised, Karl opened up, and saw a Kenyan standing outside with dusters and brooms.

"Please, sir," the man said. "I have to clean now."

Karl picked up his few things and headed back to his seat. The caterers were carrying food aboard in cartons and there were other people wandering about. Karl sat down and checked to see if he still had all his photographic equipment. His 35 mm camera and movie camera were still there, intact, under his seat, so he got up and moved across the aisle to a window. At Frankfurt he had been allocated a window seat, but had crossed the aisle to spread out for the night. Now, with luck, he might get some aerial shots of Mount Kilimanjaro. Nancy sat down beside him and they waited together for the take-off.

Renate Kahn used the stopover to stretch her legs. While she was strolling about she was surprised to see "Mickey Mouse" Helge Nachtsheim still on board.

"I thought the crew changed here in Nairobi?" Renate said.

Helge Nachtsheim nodded. "The regular crew does. But I'm only the 'Mickey Mouse' and I've got to fly all the way to Johannesburg. I'm not really a member of the crew."

"That's a long trip."

"Yes, it is," the children's stewardess agreed. "But I don't really mind. And I have my husband with me this time."

Renate watched Helge walk back down to the tail compartment. She appeared tired, and Renate thought, she must have had a long and busy night.

Hans Neeb had intended heading back to continue his business discussion with Anthony Grant in the rear section of the jumbo during the stopover. But he never got there. As he stood in the open doorway, breathing in the cool early morning air, he heard a voice he recognised. He looked behind him and saw a German business colleague, Dr Gerd Kampf-Emden. The two men shook hands, surprised and pleased to see each other. Dr Kampf-Emden was flying first class to Johannesburg to take up his new position as the managing director of a German company.

They discussed working in Africa and Hans Neeb was enthusiastic. Dr Kampf-Emden would find it most enjoyable, he predicted, and it was not as far from Europe as it seemed — just an overnight flight away. You could leave your office in Germany in the afternoon, Hans Neeb said, sleep on the jet, arrive in Johannesburg shortly before midday and still manage to get in a good afternoon's work.

They chatted on, watching the airport workmen

fussing over the 747, and made an arrangement to meet again in Johannesburg.

Elinor Senkler stood at the doorway and looked out at Africa for the first time. She saw grey clouds with the sun struggling through, a vast flat landscape of dull grass and small thorn trees and, way off in the distance, a few taller trees.

She was surprised by what she saw. It did not fit with the mental picture she had of Africa. Somehow she had thought it would be greener, the vegetation denser and more like a jungle, but here it was flat, open grassland, verging on semi-desert . . . and this was Nairobi, right on the equator, where it was supposed to rain all the year round.

She looked round to see what others were making of it and saw fellow-travellers Alfred and Veronica Solibakke seated not far away in the quiet compartment of the economy section. Veronica Solibakke was standing over her husband, combing out his thinning hair. Elinor watched, smiling. It was the sort of peaceful, domestic scene one expected to see at home, not in a jumbo jet, far away on the apron of an African airport.

I was sitting in my seat, loosely strapped in, staring at the activity around us, when the "Mickey Mouse" children's stewardess hurried past, heading towards the nose of the aircraft. She went out of sight, but reappeared a few minutes later, carrying something in the palm of her hand. When she saw us, she stopped in the aisle and smiled.

"Would your two boys like to come to the back and sit with the other children? I'll be reading a story after the take-off."

I looked at Garett. "Would you like that?"

Garett shook his head and said quietly, "No thanks, I want to stay here."

"No?" The children's stewardess smiled down at him, and he shook his head again. She looked across at Brendon, but he was sprawled back, asleep, with his head against the window, surrounded by pillows and an airline blanket.

We both laughed quietly and Lynn, speaking across the aisle, said apologetically, "I'm sorry, but they're very attached to us."

"That's quite all right," the children's stewardess said and gave a little wave as she began walking towards the back of the jet. "Enjoy your flight."

We lapsed into a sleepy silence. I looked out to my left, saw the fuel line attached to the wing, and the men working out there, with the red Nairobi Airport Fire Brigade tender close by, and felt fear in my stomach. All that fuel going in, and here we sat. All it needed was a spark and this machine would explode like a bomb. I felt so terribly vulnerable and insignificant, watching the figures through the thin window pane beyond my sleeping son. My mouth felt dry. I looked across at Lynn and smiled.

"It's damned hot."

She nodded.

I unbuckled my seat belt, stood up and placed my jacket in the overhead locker. In the pockets were my passport, a notebook and pens. I took two small pillows from the locker, dropped one onto Garett's legs, kept one, and snapped the locker shut. Brendon didn't need one; he already had two pillows *and* a blanket.

"What's this for?" Garett asked.

"For take-off," I said. "In case we bump our heads."

I strapped him in, arranged the pillow on his knees, and sat back to buckle myself in. I pulled the belt tight, very tight, the pillow resting on my thighs.

Nothing to do but wait. I reached out for the safety instruction sheet kept in the string bag fastened to the seatback in front of me and studied the position of the emergency exits. It was something I did before each take-off.

I returned the safety sheet to its place and leaned back in my seat. My palms were sweating on the pillow.

Margaret Hooker and Carol Mall climbed up the mobile steps and entered the aircraft. A stewardess showed them to their places in the front row of the economy seats, immediately behind the first class compartment, and they settled themselves and strapped in for take-off. They were in a three-seater, Margaret right up against the left-side window, a vacant seat between them, and Carol on the aisle.

Back in the airport terminal, the man allocating seats had glanced at the diagram showing him the vacant places and had given them two numbers. Then he had hesitated.

"Wait a minute," he said. "Would you two ladies like to sit together?"

"Yes," they said, because they had already struck up a conversation and seemed to get on well together.

The airline man looked back at his plan.

"As close to the toilet as possible," Carol said. "I've got an awful stomach bug."

"I think we can manage something." He gave them two new numbers and when they got on board they found they were only about two steps away from the first class toilet cabinets.

Up in the cockpit, Captain Krack and his two flight deck colleagues were planning the take-off, while the ground crew down below pumped in the last of the 61,000 kilograms (134,481 lbs) of fuel the 747 would carry.

There were 157 people on board, including the

crew, as well as a quantity of freight and baggage, making up a total estimated take-off weight of 254,576 kilograms (561,236 lbs) — well below the aircraft's maximum authorised level. Because of this, the commander decided to follow the usual practice of planning a take-off using reduced engine power. The throttle setting would be -3A power. This setting meant that *Hessen* would need 2,484 metres (2,717 yards) of runway for its take-off roll if it used runway 06, or 2,789 metres (3,051 yards) if it used runway 24.

Nairobi Airport had a single asphalt runway designated 06/24. The length was 4,117 metres (4,504 yards) and the aircraft could take off safely in either direction. Runway 24, the direction to be used by *Hessen*, had an average uphill slope of 0.4 per cent. Using this runway and -3A power, the maximum permissible take-off weight would have been approximately 284,000 kilograms (626,108 lbs).

Co-pilot Schacke, sitting in the right-hand pilot's seat, began reading the cockpit and preliminary checklists, with the various crew members responding. He would be the handling pilot for the Nairobi-Johannesburg sector.

Next to him sat Captain Krack, who was wearing his bi-focals. Krack had taken off from Nairobi ten times before and knew the airport well. He was one of Lufthansa's most experienced pilots, transferring to the airline in 1957 after serving as a pilot in the Federal Air Force. Initially, he flew as a co-pilot, and later as a captain on Lockheed 1049 and Convair 440 aircraft, and switched to Boeing 707s and 727s in 1966. In May 1972 he was checked out as a captain of Boeing 747 aircraft and had flown 1,619 hours in them. His total flying experience was 10,464 hours, and about 8,000 of those hours had been flown as a commander.

At 7.42 am the engines were started using a revised procedure the airline had introduced late in 1973. The bleed valves, which pass air from the engines to the pneumatic system to extend the leading edge flaps, were to be switched to the closed position. Once the engines had started, the flight engineer had to re-open the bleed valves to restore the power, so that it could automatically extend the leading edge flaps when the co-pilot selected them to move into the take-off position.

Fully extended leading edge flaps are almost essential for a successful take-off at high-altitude airports like Nairobi. They increase the curve and area of the wings and help to create the "lift" that enables an aircraft to overcome the pull of gravity.

On this Wednesday morning, making the after-start check, with the engines roaring, co-pilot Schacke called out, "Bleed valves."

There was a short pause and Flight Engineer Hahn

answered, "Open," signifying that he had also checked the indicator lights on his panel which showed the position of the valves.

This was the expected response, and the check continued normally.

The passengers who boarded in Nairobi had stowed away their hand luggage and were strapping in for the flight to Johannesburg. The newcomers were easily identified by their bright, lively conversation, and the restless, upright way they sat: fidgeting, looking about, trying out the push-buttons on the armrests. By contrast, those who had boarded in Frankfurt were sprawled back in their seats, dozing fitfully, their belts buckled, trying to catch up on the sleep they had lost during the night.

With the newcomers from Nairobi on board, steward Tom Scott closed the door next to him, swung the handle and sealed it. He made his checks, felt satisfied, and sat down on his seat. The jumbo was vibrating gently.

At 7.48½ am the control tower called to the *Hessen* crew, "Lufthansa five four zero. Nairobi Tower."

"Five four zero," co-pilot Schacke acknowledged. "Go ahead."

"Roger. You may take runway two-four at your discretion, or runway zero-six. Your choice."

"Oh-two-four, okay?" Captain Krack said. Using runway 24 would give *Hessen* a shorter flight path to the final track to Johannesburg.

"We take two-four," Schacke informed the tower.

"Roger. Cleared to taxi holding point, runway two-four."

"Roger," the co-pilot said into his microphone. "We are cleared to holding point, runway two-four. Are we cleared to enter?"

Captain Krack made some comment that was later indecipherable on the flight recorder.

Then at 7.49½ am the tower broke in, "Lufthansa five four zero. That is approved. Enter and backtrack."

"Roger. Thanks," co-pilot Schacke said. "So, the flaps."

"Yes," the commander agreed.

There was a chattering noise as the co-pilot set the flaps to the 10 degrees take-off position. On a normal flight, this lowering of the trailing edge flaps would automatically have signalled the vital leading edge flaps to extend. But if the bleed valves were closed there would be no pneumatic power to make this happen.

"So, that goes out pretty straight."

The flight crew spoke briefly about the weather, but the cockpit's four-channel voice recorder struggled to pick up their voices through the area microphone in the roof. The other three channels were linked to the individual crew members' intercom phones, which they were not using, because they preferred speaking directly to one another. There was no regulation requiring the crew to use the intercom, and normally this would not have caused any difficulty. The only difficulty arose because of what happened in the next few minutes.

When accident investigators tried to reconstruct the sequence of events in the cockpit, they discovered that the area microphone provided the only record of the crew's conversation. Much of this was distorted and inaudible due to noise and the distance of the crew members from the microphone. The transcript, on which this account is based, nevertheless formed part of the official East African Community report.

A short time after the brief discussion about the weather, First Officer Schacke was heard to ask the commander, "So, shall I do the rowing? [handle the take-off]"

Captain Krack replied, "Yes, please."

The aircraft turned left out of taxiway C and began backtracking slowly down the runway towards the stopway at the end, where it would turn 180 degrees and begin its take-off roll.

Sitting in the centre section between the wings, Hermann Hennecke decided to change to a window seat for the take-off. I might see something of Nairobi and the National Park, he thought, looking to his right, where there were empty seats.

He got up, still holding his paperback novel, and crossed the aisle to a seat next to the window and sat down. He had left all his other belongings on his centre row seat. He would be gone only a few minutes, he reasoned, and would move back after take-off; nothing could possibly happen to his things in that short time.

Hennecke took up the end of the seat belt, slipped it through the grip, and pulled it tight, *very tight*, an unusual action for him. Usually, when he flew, he simply hooked the belt up loosely, because the airline insisted on passengers wearing one, but today he wore it tightly against his stomach.

He glanced up the aisle towards the nose and saw the stewardess settling herself on her doorway seat, only four rows ahead of him. Then he turned back and stared out of the window. The jumbo jet was taxiing smoothly out of the service area. The engines and the starboard wing angled back, and he could see the runway rolling by slowly beneath the jet. I should see everything from here, he thought.

Right in the front of the aircraft, in row 1 in the first class section, it seemed to Bob Laburn that *Hessen* was moving again rather soon after the new crew had boarded. Usually there was a long delay out on the apron, but on this morning everything seemed to be happening quickly.

As the 747 rolled on, he heard a woman's voice speaking over the public address system. All seat belts should be fastened, the voice said, and there should be no smoking during take-off.

"We wish you a pleasant flight."

And then there was only the muffled noise of the engines and the slight bobbing motion of the aircraft.

In the cockpit, immediately above the first class passenger cabin, Flight Engineer Rudi Hahn sat looking towards the nose of the 747. His seat was in the forward position, and he was preparing to read the taxiing checklist. The big jet trundled slowly down the runway towards its turning point, engines roaring.

"Checklist," he called out. "Brakes."

"Are checked."

"Flaps," Rudi Hahn called out.

A different voice, probably Captain Krack's, responded, "Ten ten," followed by another word, which may have been "green." Both the flight engineer and the commander were expected to respond, but the voice recorder failed to pick up a response from Rudi Hahn. This may have been due to the limitations of the area microphone in the cockpit ceiling.

This was the vital check, which should have revealed that the leading edge flaps were not extended. In making it, the flight engineer was required to check two double filament lights on the right hand side of the pilot's main centre instrument panel, one green and one amber, and then check two rows of eight double-bulb lights, one row green and the other amber, on the extreme right hand side of the flight engineer's panel.

The lights were arranged in pairs, one amber paired with one green. What Flight Engineer Hahn was looking for was a green light on the pilot's panel, and eight green lights on his own panel. This would mean that all the leading edge flaps were fully extended. If any of the green lights were unlit, or if an amber light was burning, it would indicate that the flaps were not correctly positioned, and take-off should not be attempted.

The crew members involved believed they had seen the correct combination of green lights, so the checklist reading continued.

"Flight controls," the flight engineer called out.

The answer was indistinct.

"Yaw dampers." There was a pause, then, "Checked."

"Flight instruments and annunciator panels," Rudi Hahn called out.

"No warnings," said Captain Krack.

"No warnings here," reported co-pilot Schacke.

Flight Engineer Hahn read off a succession of items, pausing as he checked each and gave his response.

"APU."

"Off. Door closed."

"Fuel temperature and heater."

"Checked and closed."

"Fuel panel and pressure."

"Checked. Pumps on."

"Cabin report."

"Not yet."

"Cockpit door is open."

"Stabiliser and trim."

Captain Krack made an incomprehensible comment.

"Stabiliser trim," First Officer Schacke reported, and the rest was drowned by noise.

"Good."

"Yes."

"Rudder and aileron trim," Flight Engineer Hahn called out.

"Zero here, zero there," co-pilot Schacke reported.

"Yes," confirmed Captain Krack.

"Yes," the flight engineer agreed. "Take-off data."

"Yes," the co-pilot said, and began reading off a series of numerical values which the microphone had difficulty in picking up, while in the background Flight Engineer Hahn could be heard talking to Purser Heidi Tischer.

Captain Krack called out, "Cabin report received."

"Checklist completed," Flight Engineer Hahn

reported.

The jumbo jet had reached the end of the runway and Captain Krack began the turn into the stopway. At 7.51 am the control tower broke in, "Lufthansa five four zero, your clearance."

"Go ahead," co-pilot Schacke said.

"ATC clears Lufthansa five four zero Nairobi to Jan Smuts [Johannesburg] delta amber one zero," the tower advised. "Climb and maintain flight level three five zero to Mike Bravo Mbeya echo departure and check clearance expires at five six. Time now is five one."

In the economy class compartment between the wings, businessman Terry Partridge, from Sheffield, England, came to the end of the last page of the book he had been reading, closed it and placed it in the seat pocket in front of him. It was nicely timed. The jumbo was making its turn at the head of the runway and he shifted so he could watch the take-off through the window, one seat away to his right.

He was sitting almost exactly halfway down the aircraft. There was only one row of seats behind him and then came the midway gap for the emergency door that led out over the wing. He felt comfortable and relaxed. The flight so far had been smooth and trouble-free and, for a man who averaged a hundred to a hundred and fifty flights a year, it seemed to be just another ordinary trip, like setting off in a car, or bus.

He stared out and had that familiar sensation of the world outside wheeling slowly around as the 747 turned 180 degrees in the stopway, and lined up for the take-off roll.

Captain Krack had completed the turn and *Hessen* faced south down runway 24. "We are ready to go," he said.

"So, let us do the check," co-pilot Schacke called out.

Flight Engineer Hahn began reading the take-off checklist, "So, landing lights."

"Normal, on," responded Captain Krack.

At 7.52½ am a voice from the control tower interrupted: "Lufthansa five four zero cleared for take-off. Surface wind calm."

"Transponder," Rudi Hahn challenged.

"Roger," one of the pilots answered the control tower. "Cleared for take-off."

"Transponder," Rudi Hahn repeated.

"We don't have one," the co-pilot replied.

"Pack valves closed. Ignition is on. Body gear steering."

"Disarmed," said Captain Krack.

"Take-off checklist is completed," Flight Engineer Hahn reported.

"Okay," co-pilot Schacke acknowledged. He spoke briefly with the commander, but there was too much noise. The microphone was overwhelmed.

Captain Krack partially opened the throttles, co-pilot Schacke took control of the nosewheel steering and the noise level increased as the roll began.

Behind them, Rudi Hahn adjusted the throttles to the correct -3A take-off power. *Hessen*'s tyres were spinning over the hard surface as the speed built up. The seconds ticked by. Ten . . . fifteen . . . twenty . . .

Twenty-four seconds after the roll had begun, Schacke called out, "Eighty."

Captain Krack began speaking, "Yes . . . " But the rest of his speech was drowned by noise.

Hessen's indicated airspeed was touching eighty knots and Rudi Hahn gave over control of the throttles to Captain Krack, but remained sitting forward so he could check the instruments on the pilot's centre panel.

"Okay," the commander said.

The speed built up steadily, the take-off run normal, thrust adequate and no evidence of excessive drag. They were hurtling along the runway, approaching their target speed of 135 to 136 knots.

Thirty-eight seconds into the roll one of the pilots called out, "V1." (V1 is the point at which an aircraft reaches its take-off speed and the pilot must decide whether or not to attempt the take-off.)

In the next five seconds, shortly before *Hessen* reached its target rotation speed (VR), co-pilot Schacke eased his forward pressure on the control column.

"VR," a voice called out.

The co-pilot began the rotation, and *Hessen*'s nosewheel lifted smoothly about ten degrees from the runway. The aircraft's acceleration ended suddenly. For the next seven or eight seconds the jet rushed along nose-up at about 145 knots. The main wheels lifted somewhere between 2,500 and 3,000 yards down the runway, and *Hessen* rose slowly into the air. As the aircraft was lifting off, the three men in the cockpit saw birds flying past the nose.

Hessen climbed sluggishly at about 450 feet a minute. Far too slow. Normally the aircraft would have been climbing at 1,500 to 1,800 feet per minute, and the airspeed would have increased dramatically as the jumbo surged out of "ground effect." But on this take-off *Hessen*'s speed did not rise above 145 knots.

And then the aircraft began to shake.

Captain Krack called out urgently, "Pay attention. Vibration . . . " his voice fading in the noise. He turned quickly to Rudi Hahn and asked if there were any signs of abnormal engine vibration. Some of the birds they had seen may have been sucked into the engines.

The flight engineer looked at his panel, checked

the meters and warning lights. He reported, "All is OK."

"Vibration," Captain Krack repeated, puzzled. Then he thought, it might be caused by unbalanced wheels. He checked the instruments, saw they indicated a positive rate of climb, and initiated retraction of the four large clusters of wheels and the nosewheel.

"Gear up," co-pilot Schacke called out.

There was a metallic click as the lever went home and the cycle began.

Flying along at 143 knots, *Hessen's* landing gear doors began opening to receive the wheels. The action added to the drag at a critical moment. The airspeed was cut by about 40 feet a minute.

If the wheels could be lifted in time, and the protruding doors closed, the aircraft's speed should increase by about 100 feet a minute. But on this morning the undercarriage, which normally took about twenty-one seconds to raise, was still partly extended when *Hessen* struck the ground.

"Gear travelling," co-pilot Schacke reported.

It was eighteen seconds before impact.

Hessen had reached 100 feet above the ground. The rate of climb, which had started out at between 400 and 500 feet a minute, fell suddenly to zero.

Co-pilot Schacke lost all feeling of acceleration. He was forced to lower the nose to prevent the airspeed from dropping below 140 knots.

The 747 began sinking gradually towards the earth.

"Engines okay so far," Flight Engineer Hahn called out.

Captain Krack acknowledged.

Six seconds passed.

"RPM is also okay," Hahn informed the commander.

There was a harsh rattle as the control column shook, warning the crew of an approaching stall.

"Stickshaker," the flight engineer called out.

The automatic warning system rattled on for three seconds. *Hessen*'s speed fell dangerously to 140 knots.

Captain Krack quickly placed his hands on the control column to lower the nose. But the aircraft was too close to the ground. There was no room to manoeuvre.

"Okay, crash!" co-pilot Schacke broke in.

Through their headphones, the crew could hear the control tower trying to summon the firefighting crews: "Fire Station Tower!"

The stickshaker rattled again.

"Fire Station Tower!"

The ground came up to meet them.

In the last second, co-pilot Schacke closed all four throttles. The automatic warning horn, designed to prevent flying crews from landing with their wheels up, began to sound.

5 • 'Fire Station Tower!'

A small French car carrying three passengers and a load of luggage turned off the Nairobi-Mombasa road and headed towards Nairobi's international airport. Driving the car was author and animal conservationist Jock Leslie-Melville, who also managed a photographic safari company. He was taking his stepdaughter, Dancy Bruce, and her friend, Esther Burton, to the airport to board a charter flight to London, where Dancy worked for an antiques dealer.

They had been told to check in at eight that morning but, knowing what charter flights could be like, they had planned to get there fifteen minutes early. They were a few minutes later than planned, but still early for check-in, and driving along steadily, the tyres swishing through puddles of overnight rain, the windows rolled up to keep out the chill of the early morning air. The clouds were thinning, and ahead of them, down the airport road, they could see pale sunshine touching on the terminal building. Beyond the blurred yellow-brown grass, about four hundred yards to their right, stretched the dark ribbon of the airport runway.

Sitting in the front passenger seat alongside Jock Leslie-Melville, Dancy was staring at the vegetation they were passing. She knew, deep down, that after a few weeks in London, she would be feeling homesick for all that she was seeing: the waving grass, the broad plains and hugeness of the sky, the sense of vast openness and space that was Africa. But in that strange conflict of emotions that travellers often experience, she was, at the same time, looking forward to being back in the whirl and tumult of big-city London.

In a few hours she would be walking down London's streets. But until she arrived, she would pay heavily in nervous tension: Dancy hated flying. Already that familiar ball of knotted nerves was throbbing in her stomach, and her mouth felt dry. Thankfully, this time she would have the company of Esther Burton to distract her; friendly Esther who, before this morning, had not even seen a jumbo jet, but had a secret ambition to fly in one.

And then, as they rolled along the road, Dancy saw a jumbo jet. It was in the air above the runway, its dark nose aimed upwards, the sun reflecting off the tail, and Dancy called out, "Look over there, Esther. That's your 747."

Esther sat up and looked out. And Jock turned his

eyes from the road to watch. The huge jet seemed to be heading directly towards them, moving slowly, and strangely. Very strangely. Nose-up, tail-down.

"But what's it doing?" Esther asked.

"It must be landing."

"It can't be," Jock said. "It's already past the runway."

Jock and Dancy stared at the jet and realised something was wrong: the 747 was not climbing. And it was not landing. It was flying along, now directly in line with them.

Jock swung the car off the road and stopped, almost without realising what he was doing.

"It's crashing," Dancy said.

But she didn't, couldn't believe what she had just said. Then she thought, maybe they've forgotten a passenger, or they're having some sort of trouble and they're turning back. It can't *really* crash.

But the aircraft went on drifting slowly down, down, down. No sounds or noise filtered through the rolled-up car windows. It was like a silent movie. The aircraft went towards the muddy earth, a giant modern airliner, gleaming in the soft morning sunshine. At the last moment it dropped below the horizon. A split second later there was a flash. Flames shot skywards. A great expanding fireball rose above the bush and clouds of black and dense brown smoke billowed into the blue. The smoke twisted into a towering mushroom, swirling and turning.

"Oh, God," Esther said.

Dancy reeled back. She felt ill. All those people. Nobody could get out of a thing like that.

There was silence in the car. The three of them sat, shocked beyond words, while the smoke rose higher and higher.

The watchroom attendant at the airport fire brigade tower watched, horrified, as the big jet appeared to falter in the air beyond the end of runway 24. He reached out and sounded the alarm bell. It rang loudly, startling the duty crews into action. As it did so, the officer continued watching, unable to look away. The aircraft was struggling on, nose-up, but dropping steadily.

The duty crews grabbed their helmets and held on as the fire tenders swung out onto the runway. They raced on behind the stricken aircraft, motors roaring, the shrill note of the sirens rising and falling. Ahead of the firemen the 747 was still flying, but dropping lower.

The tail brushed some bushes. Seconds later, it struck the ground, scraping along for about a hundred yards. Directly in the 747's path was an embanked road. There was a flash of flame as the engines on the left wing and the rear fuselage slammed into the earthwork. Pieces of metal flew off. Shattered by the impact, the tail section and rear fuselage broke off behind the wings and began disintegrating, hurling out passengers and crew. Fire flared up.

The forward section bounced off the road surface into the air, shedding engines and an outer section of the left wing, and came crashing back down. For the next 350 yards it skidded across the muddy earth, left wing blazing, then swung almost 180 degrees and slid back towards the embanked road. Thick mud slowed and finally stopped the headlong thrust. *Hessen* came to rest, leaning to the left, the rear section missing from behind the wings, the front section below the cockpit twisted and cracked.

The oncoming firemen saw dark, oily smoke shooting skywards on the far side of the embankment. The fire tenders were unable to get over the eight-foot embankment. They braked and swung away sharply, heading for an emergency fire breakout road that would bring them close to the wreckage. Sirens screaming, they roared along it. Suddenly, they found their progress impeded by the vehicles of hundreds of sightseers.

Riding in one of the fire tenders was Lufthansa's security man, Norbert Diekmann. He had been on duty in the service area during the refuelling stop and had turned to watch the 747's take-off roll, fascinated even after all this time that an aircraft so huge could lift itself off the ground.

He had watched it thundering down the runway,

saw the nosewheel lift and the jet rise slowly into the air until it was about 100 feet off the ground. Then he and the refuelling crew had watched, shocked, as it came back to earth, still moving forward, nose up.

They saw a flash as the aircraft crashed into the embanked road, and Diekmann heard a blast, followed by another, as the 747 lurched over the top. He began running blindly towards the burning jumbo, holding his hat under his arm.

As he ran, Diekmann felt sick at heart. All his friends were on board that aircraft and he feared he might never see any of them again.

Back on the airfield, the control tower's urgent calls to the fire station tower had gone unanswered.

Suddenly there was a torrent of unintelligible words from one of the fire brigade vehicles. All the control tower could hear were the words "aircraft", more noises, and "fire".

A voice from the fire station broke in, "Ah, Tower. Fire Station."

"Station, go ahead," the tower instructed.

"Up till now there has not been any outside aid. The jumbo Lufthansa is . . . on fire," the fire station reported.

"Roger," the control tower acknowledged. "One five seven on board. One five seven."

Three and a half minutes after the jet had struck the

embanked road the fire station called the control tower again: "Would you inform the Airport Authority to come and assist the fire."

"Will you say again please, Fire Station," the tower instructed.

"Will you assist the . . . the . . . the fire people to the . . . to the incident of the accident just at the . . . " the words ran together, " . . . zero six."

"Fire Station, from Tower. You are unreadable. Would you please say again slowly."

"I say again. The jumbo jet is on fire and up to now there's been no outside aid."

"Roger. Roger," control tower said. "We are doing it right now."

"Exchange seems to be asleep," the fire station commented.

"Roger."

The fire station broke in: "If you can get hold of the Ministry of Works yard, will you inform them to despatch some of their lorries to come and take the crews out to the incident of the accident."

"Roger. Will do that."

The control tower tried to contact the fire brigade vehicles speeding to the accident. "Fire Seven, confirm you are at the scene of the fire."

The fire station replied, "Affirmative." Because of the crowds and traffic and difficult terrain, it had taken the firemen almost five minutes to get to the crash site.

One of the vehicles answered. "Control Tower, this is Fire One. Do you read?"

"Fire One, go ahead."

"Will you ask the City Fire Brigade and Kenya Air Force for additional fire appliances bringing water, bringing water."

"Roger. Will do."

The voice came again, "Nairobi Tower, Fire One."

"Fire One, go ahead."

"Would you please immediately contact outside aids, outside aids. Over."

"We just asked for them," the control tower reported.

There was a jumble of words and a voice from Fire One at the scene of the wreck pleaded, "Send them immediately, because the scene is horrible."

6 • *Take-off and impact*

The roll began almost immediately. There was no long wait at the head of the runway, no revving of engines. The big jet completed its turn and off we went. The engines were thrusting us along, the huge tyres spinning over ridges and puddles. I looked left. The runway and grass were beginning to blur. But I felt uneasy. Too slow, I thought. Too slow. We'll never make it.

I looked to the right, past Lynn sitting across the aisle, past the rows and rows of seats, and saw the airport buildings drawing level, and I felt through the seat with my whole body every bump, jump, leap and lurch as we rolled down the runway. Then I thought, stop it, stop panicking. It always feels too slow, and you always make it.

I looked left again, saw the wildly rushing grass, the whole world going madly by and thought, see, we *are* going fast enough. We *will* make it.

Hermann Hennecke felt the jumbo rolling on and on and on. At first he felt the thrust of acceleration. And then he had a feeling the speed had fallen. The 747 was not going fast enough for take-off.

My God, he thought as the jet thundered on, we must be nearing the end of the runway and we haven't taken off yet!

Steward Tom Scott, sitting strapped in next to Jürgen Freund with his back to the nose, could see the ground hurtling away behind the aircraft as the speed built up and felt himself bowing slightly with the acceleration. He had flown many hours as a pilot in the United States and knew all about take-offs and aerodynamics, and so far he was happy. Everything seemed to be going along smoothly. He estimated they would soon be coming up to the velocity rotation point, the point at which the speed is just right and the pilot pulls back on the control column, swinging the elevators up in the tail, causing the tail to press down, and the nose wheel to lift off the runway.

There it was. The lift. Now after three or four seconds, when the angle was right, the jumbo should rise steadily and smoothly into the air, climbing solidly away with a thrust that would press the passengers back against their seats.

But in that instant after rotation, Tom Scott felt something odd. The wheels bounced. A short, sharp bounce. He had never felt that before and thought, that's strange, something's not right. We aren't climbing fast enough.

Ah, Hermann Hennecke thought, I was wrong. The jumbo has enough power after all. The pilot's made it, we're off the ground, and everything's fine.

Still strapped in, he reached out for his detective novel, and at that moment everything began to shake. Things leaped up and jumped about. It sounded as if the aircraft was breaking up. He looked out and saw the wing tip swinging in a huge arc.

A few rows away, American sisters Tillie Harmel and Gladys Golman had clasped hands across the aisle, as they always did when flying together. They could see the skyline changing as the jet rose slowly.

The angle of the skyline changed abruptly and the aircraft shuddered. Something was terribly wrong with it. The sisters looked at each other in alarm, and their clasp tightened.

We knew, when the violent shuddering began, that we were flying in a doomed aircraft. On the wings the engines were shaking in their mountings and there was a loud metallic coughing. I looked across the aisle at Lynn and thought, this is it.

A glass of orange juice leaped off the seat tray next to her. Lynn grabbed at it. She caught the glass, but the juice flew on up, drenching her hair.

The jumbo was struggling away from the runway. There was none of that thrusting power we had felt in Frankfurt. We were up about a hundred feet and, looking down, I saw the ground staying the same distance away.

Tom Scott looked out of the window and saw the wing jerking wildly and condensation streaming over the top. He couldn't understand it. There was no reason for the shaking. There was no wind, and they were still so low they should have been protected from any gusts. And that condensation . . . it shouldn't be that wet out there over the wings.

In the few seconds that it took to notice this, Tom Scott realised that the aircraft was stalling. He couldn't believe it. With all the precautions the airline took, with all the built-in safety devices of the 747, how could it possibly happen?

After twenty seconds of flight, as the jumbo continued shuddering through the air, he thought, we're too low. Far, far too low. We're about a hundred feet off the ground. At this point we should be at least a thousand feet up, and climbing.

At that moment he knew they would crash. They would come hurtling back down, and he knew from statistics that he wouldn't survive, that few people ever survived stall accidents on take-off at such a low altitude. They would plough back into the earth and all of them would be killed.

Thoughts raced through his mind, spurred by the realisation that everything would soon be blotted out, that his life was nearly over. Why, he thought, why do I have to be on this plane? I wish I was sitting up in that cockpit. At least I wish I knew what's causing that stall. What is happening up there? Do they know?

Beyond the windows, he could see the wing still shaking. They were coming down. Tom Scott pressed his head back against the seat, closed his eyes and thought about his family, what they would have to go through because of this, how his wife Alexandra, back home in Bad Soden, near Frankfurt, would feel when they told her. He didn't want to see the end. He kept his eyes shut and gripped tightly on the seat. Any second now. He wondered what it would feel like to hit the ground, if he would live through the impact, if it would be a slow death.

"We're not gaining altitude fast enough," Karl Kahn yelled to his daughter Nancy. He did a lot of flying on business in the United States, but this take-off was unlike anything he had ever experienced — shaking and shuddering, and a frightening lack of thrust.

Nancy nudged him. "That looks like smoke."

He looked out and, to him, it seemed like low hanging cloud. The jumbo passed through it.

"Cloud," he said.

Hermann Hennecke stared in disbelief at the muddy earth. The big jet couldn't be coming down. They would pull out of it, they *had* to. They would pull out of it and this terrible shaking would stop.

Then he saw the ground coming closer, and he knew suddenly that they would not.

"This is the end," John Bing thought as the shaking worsened. Loose objects were flying about the cabin, lockers were snapping open; blankets, briefcases and packages came tumbling down.

"Let it be painless," he said to himself. "Please let it be painless."

Up in the nose, Bob Laburn felt the jumbo shuddering. The man next to him put his head on his knees. Bob glanced quickly at him, and did the same. The emergency instructions, he thought, but who ever remembers them?

A few seats away, Malcolm Solts felt the aircraft losing all power and sensed that something awful was going to happen. They were being hurled backwards and forwards, with only the seat belts keeping them in their seats. He reached up, snatched his glasses off his face, and threw them on the floor, and rolled himself up with his head on his knees.

We had passed the end of the runway. Now, below us, was only rough bush. The 747 began to lose height, still struggling along, nose-up. We were going in. The fears of a lifetime had become reality, but my mind refused to accept it. No, I argued desperately, we can't crash, I don't want us to crash. We've got our whole lives ahead of us, there's still so much I want to do, and those two sons of ours . . . why did I bring them with me?

I stared out of the window, anguished, unable to react, sensing death ahead and feeling an icy cold shiver ran up my back. The ground came closer.

"Put your head down!" my wife Lynn shouted, and I pulled Garett down so his head was on his knees. Brendon was still sleeping, sprawled back in his seat. I tried, but couldn't reach him. It was unearthly inside the jet. No one screamed. No one shouted to us to do anything. There was only that mechanical coughing, the sound of things crashing about, objects falling. Some passengers were still sitting erect in their seats.

Garett shifted his head to look.

"Stay down!" I shouted, pushing at him.

I saw the nun in the row ahead bow her head. I ducked.

Alarmed, Elinor Senkler tapped her husband's shoulder and asked, "Are we in trouble?"

Former Royal Canadian Air Force pilot Edmund

Senkler stared out of his port side window and saw the engines shaking on the wing. This is a pre-stall flutter, he realised. How is our pilot going to stop us from going into a spin? His wartime training came back to him: pull back on the throttles, and drop the nose.

He felt *Hessen*'s nose had dropped and was relieved. We'll glide in for an emergency landing in this flat field, come to a stop and climb out.

The aircraft sank lower. Out of nowhere, an embanked earth road loomed up. Edmund Senkler realised they were heading straight for it.

At the last moment steward Tom Scott felt the engines throttling back to idle and thought, oh great, the captain's found a field or some place to set the plane down. We might get out of this after all.

On the other side of the cabin, Hermann Hennecke stretched his arms out in front of him and dropped his head. There was a sickening crash as some part of the machine struck. He was hurled against his seat belt. There were no screams, no shouts, nothing, as the 747 bounced across the earth, seats breaking loose, luggage coming down from the overhead lockers. And then the lights went out.

Margaret Hooker and Carol Mall had been chatting during the take-off. As the nose lifted, Carol put her hand up to her face and took off her glasses. At the same time, Margaret remembered her husband telling her he had seen animals on the ground once, while taking off from Nairobi, and she turned her head, thinking, I'll look and see if I can see any. She was so intent on the bush that she did not notice the earth coming rapidly closer.

There was a flash, and they were scraping the ground. It was so quick, like being in the centre of an explosion, a tremendous concussion, and Margaret felt she was somersaulting. She and the seat and Carol were going through the air together. An unbelievable sensation. Unreal. They crashed down through the floor, but she felt no pain, nothing at all. The jumbo had cracked open and they dropped through into the dark of the baggage hold below.

Edmund Senkler, still sitting upright and staring out of the window, felt a jarring blow in his back. He was thrown forward as the tail slammed into the ground in front of the road. The jumbo reared up, bouncing over the embankment. He saw sparks flying past the window and heard metal tearing somewhere behind him. Pieces of plastic from the ceiling hurtled past his head.

Then the jet struck again.

Passengers in the first class compartment heard a wrenching sound. Bob Laburn lifted his head to see what had happened, and everything went black.

My head smashed against the seat in front of me. Rows of seats tore loose from the floor and folded forward like a pack of cards. We were trapped in between, strapped to our row of three joined seats, and my feet were pressing against the heaving floor to keep us upright. My face was twisted to the left and I saw Brendon being hurled like a rag doll.

I shouted, "Are you all right? Are you all right?"

He did not answer and I thought, my God, his neck's broken.

Then we jerked again.

It felt as if we were on the ground, and sliding along. The aircraft slewed to the left. There were ripping sounds, and sections of the ceiling, lockers and luggage began falling on us. Dust filled the cabin. And we were still sliding.

I saw a fireball of flame erupting where the port wing had been. Right next to us it was all flames and thick black smoke. There was only a small sheet of glass between Brendon and the fire.

The first impact drove Tom Scott back hard against his seat, but it was only a glancing blow. The jumbo struck again, and this one really shook him up. He felt it in his back. He opened his eyes and saw the 747 was sliding along, riding over the rough ground, lurching and groaning as it broke up. Amazed that nothing was happening to him, he held on grimly, waiting as the long jarring slide continued.

On the starboard side of the economy cabin, a locker housing the crew's serving trolleys burst open, and the trolleys were flung towards stewardess Antje Kollner, seated alone near the emergency door over the wing.

The stewardess ripped off her seat belt and jumped aside. The trolleys smashed into the seat she had just left. Seconds later, the ceiling above her head shattered, and an inflatable dinghy pack tumbled down. It blocked the exit, but missed the stewardess by inches.

A row ahead of her, luggage lockers above businessman Terry Partridge's head broke off the ceiling. He raised his arm to fend off a dark object, and his briefcase and jacket fell on top of him. That damned locker. He'd had trouble earlier, keeping it shut. Now it had almost killed him.

As the jumbo bounced across the bush Terry Partridge glanced to his left. Beyond the rows of seats and windows he saw something that filled him with dread. The port wing was rubbing on the ground, and all along it flames were shooting up.

The aircraft slowed, and the force was tremendous. John Bing saw debris and loose overhead luggage change direction and fall back on top of cowering passengers. Some were struck on the head.

He was alarmed and looked across the aisle at his wife Jean. Was she all right? He saw her sitting there, three places away, gripping onto her seat. A huge section of the ceiling broke off and swung down. He watched, horrified, as it struck Jean in the chest. It must have killed her, he thought, anguished.

Malcolm Solts held on tightly, the impact hurling him against his seat belt. He heard glass breaking and metal tearing and crumpling. The inside of the aircraft seemed to be coming apart. Panels shattered and jagged sheets of plastic were flying through the air. There were bumps and awful groaning noises as the jet ploughed on. He kept his head down against his knees. Hold on, he told himself. Keep holding on.

The floor jarred and heaved and rocked beneath his feet. Things fell on him, baggage, dust, chunks of ceiling, but he held on grimly, shoulders hunched and head down, as the aircraft broke up around him.

The long, jarring slide ended abruptly. Tom Scott couldn't believe he was still alive. To his left, everything was shattered and broken. To his right, there were flames. Fire leaped up outside the exit door. Oh boy, he thought angrily, you've survived the crash, and now you'll burn to death, because you can't get out.

7 • 'Wake up, it's a crash!'

Hans Neeb felt badly shaken. But, to his amazement, he was alive. In his seat, in the quiet compartment forward of the wings, he raised his head from between his arms. The jumbo had stopped moving and he wasn't even hurt. On impact, the seats in front of him had broken off the floor and gone crashing towards the first class compartment. Dust and splintered plastic were still showering down.

He looked about, listening for voices, or cries for help. But there weren't any. The silence after the noise of the impact was unnerving. He knew he had to get out, right away.

He loosened his seat belt and stood up shakily. His eyes took in the astonishing wreckage of the cabin as he stepped into the aisle. He remembered seeing an exit somewhere to the right, a few rows from his seat, and he moved quickly in that direction, shouting, "*Raus! Raus!*" He didn't think about his luggage. All he could think about was reaching that door . . .

Hans Neeb saw the door. At almost the same moment, he saw a stewardess. She was pushing desperately at the door, struggling to get it open. But the door seemed to have jammed.

For a few seconds after the jumbo's long slide ended Hermann Hennecke sat, numbed. There was no sound from the other passengers. Was he the only one left alive? He sat listening. Suddenly, a voice shouted, "We must get out!"

Sitting confused in the half-dark, unable to think logically or understand what had happened, Hermann peered back across the aisle towards his old seat in the centre section. He couldn't see any of the other passengers who had been there only seconds before. Where were they? What had happened to them?

And then he saw small tongues of flame flickering across the collapsed ceiling edges near the back of the section he was in.

Hermann tugged at his seat belt and felt it unclasp in his hands. Four rows ahead, he picked out the bright yellow uniform of a stewardess at the exit door. She had both hands on the door handle and was pulling at it desperately, trying to get it to move. It had to turn through 180 degrees.

Unbuckled, but still too shocked to move from his seat, Hermann Hennecke kept his eyes on the woman, wondering if she had the strength to do it.

She *must* get it open, he thought. She *must*. Or we'll all die in the fire.

On the opposite side of the aircraft, steward Tom Scott sat strapped to his crew seat, shocked by the realisation that he had survived the impact, and would now burn to death instead. He spent a few angry moments thinking about it. But his mood changed abruptly. His emergency evacuation training took over.

He unbuckled his seat belt and jumped up. He had to get the surviving passengers out, and he knew, from what he had seen, that there was no way out on his side of the aircraft; they would all go straight into the fire.

He decided to try the other side. To get there, he had to go through the small kitchen where the crew heated up in-flight meals. But the kitchen was blocked. Shattered ceiling panels and toppled equipment filled the narrow passageway. Tom Scott could not see a way through.

Frantic, he ran at the wreckage, tearing and punching at it with his bare hands, using his body to shoulder it aside. He saw movement ahead and, as he pushed closer, saw stewardess Evelyn Rehm and a male passenger. They were struggling to open the exit directly in front of the right wing.

Tom Scott joined them in the doorway, and saw

in an instant that they had managed to get the door only partly open. He added his weight to their efforts and, with all three pushing, the door was forced back slowly against the fuselage, and daylight streamed in.

One moment Hermann Hennecke was sitting fixed in his seat. An instant later he was right beside the door. He did not know how he got there, but suddenly he was there, and jumping, not through a door, it seemed, but into the light. At first he was falling. Then he hit the ground and toppled forward onto his hands. There was no pain, only a feeling of immense relief. He began scrambling through the mud on his hands and knees, the first person out of the economy section.

As he crawled something struck him on the back. Horrified, Hermann thought, it's the side of the plane! It's burst open and I'm under it.

He didn't stop to look, but frantically clawed his way out from underneath the huge object, got shakily to his feet and stumbled off, half running, over the rough ground with only the open air before him. He was repeating crazily to himself, "You are out! You are out!"

Later, airline officials suggested that he had been hit by the escape chute as it inflated.

He was still running, seeing everything ahead of him as hazy and strange, when there was an explosion behind him. He turned to look at the burning jet and realised suddenly why everything seemed so odd. He had lost his glasses. But he still saw the flames, great fuzzy flames, leaping up over the wreck from which he had escaped.

In the doorway in front of the right wing the escape chute had inflated, intact and undamaged, bridging the gap between the door sill and the ground. Everything looked perfect for escape and Tom Scott's instincts screamed at him, run, get out of here as fast as you can. But he fought the impulse, telling himself, you can't do that, you've got to stay. You're a trained person and you've got to help all these people out.

He turned and began shouting in a mixture of German and English, "*Raus*! Out! *Raus*! Out!" He was amazed at the power of his voice. It did not seem as if it belonged to him, yelling out hoarsely, urgently, in the crumbling wreckage.

Most of the passengers were sitting, deeply shocked. But at the sound of his voice they seemed to come alive. They jumped up and came running towards the door, bunched together, wide-eyed and frightened.

Tom Scott grabbed them as they came, grabbed arms, shoulders, collars, jackets, shirt-sleeves, whatever he could hold, and hurled them down the escape chute. He wasn't too gentle, but he did not want any blockages in the doorway. No matter what anyone might say or think, a broken leg was better than burning horribly to death in a 747.

Out they went, most of them landing on the chute in a sitting posture, some tipping over onto their backs, and scrambling to their feet at the bottom. There was no screaming, but fear pushed some beyond normal behaviour. A woman fell down a few yards in front of the open doorway and the passengers coming on behind ran right over her.

Two rows from the door, Renate Kahn sat dazed and motionless. All she could think was, don't move, stay put until someone gives you some sort of instructions. Her gaze was fixed on the drama at the door, and she heard Tom Scott begin shouting, "*Raus*! Out!"

She responded to his command in an instant. She did not even look back to see what was happening to Karl and Nancy, sitting a few rows behind her. Renate jumped up and ran.

She reached the door and was pushed down the chute. Halfway down, she became stuck; the angle was not steep enough. She got herself moving again, using her hands and heels, stepped off into the mud, and stood next to the chute, watching for her family to appear in the doorway above her. In her shocked state it did not occur to her that the aircraft she was standing next to could explode at any second.

Inside the jumbo, Karl and Nancy Kahn had seen

Renate go. Karl threw down his camera, grabbed his daughter's arm and shouted, "Let's get out!"

Parts of the ceiling were coming down on them. Nancy snatched her glasses from the seat pocket, leaped up and ran for the door in her heavy hiking boots. Karl was right with her, and they went through the door together and down the escape chute. They slid as far as they could, got up and found Renate standing close by, looking at them.

Karl shouted, "Run! It's going to explode!" and they took off over the bush.

Behind the Kahns came the American sisters, Tillie Harmel and Gladys Golman. They were still on the chute when Karl Kahn shouted, and it terrified them. If the jumbo blew up now . . .

Halfway down, Tillie Harmel lost a shoe. She hesitated, leaned back for it, but couldn't reach it, and her sister slid past her to the ground.

Gladys Golman leaped up, grabbed Tillie roughly by the leg and pulled her down. The two sisters ran through the mud together, Tillie struggling along in one shoe.

Ahead of them, Karl Kahn was yelling, "Keep going, keep going! It's going to explode!"

Tillie Harmel stopped, took off her remaining shoe, and ran on, holding it in her hand. She was breathing harshly, mouth open from exertion, but she kept on running. She was exhausted and badly shocked, and it was a long time before she realised she had been injured.

John Bing looked through the window to his left and was horrified to see the wing on fire, the flames so close he could feel the heat. Get out of here, his instincts shouted at him. Get away from the fire. He was unstrapped in seconds, jumped up and rushed across the aisle to his wife, afraid he might find her dead.

Jean Bing was sitting surrounded by wreckage from the ceiling. John grabbed at it and was surprised by its lightness. He was relieved to see that Jean was moving and seemed unhurt.

A woman's voice was shouting, "This way! Out here!"

The voice came from the starboard side of the jumbo, and the Bings went towards the sound, away from the fire. They made their way awkwardly across the wrecked cabin, crunching over debris on the floor, protecting their heads from the dust and tumbling panels. Ahead, they saw the yellow uniform of a stewardess. There was wreckage blocking the emergency exit and the young woman was bent down, hurling it aside. The way was clear. She tugged at the handle and the door swung outwards over the wing. There were now two doors open for survivors to use.

"Out over here!" she shouted and began pushing

passengers through.

People were crowded together and lined up behind the Bings, but everyone was moving quickly. The Bings went through the exit together and found themselves walking on a half-inflated escape chute on top of the wing. The chute was not needed; the rear of the wing was touching the ground. The Bings stepped quickly over the curved surface and hopped off into the mud, followed by the others.

Someone was shouting at them to run, to get away from the burning jumbo, and the Bings ran, John in his shirtsleeves, and Jean limping along, one shoe missing.

Close behind them came businessman Terry Partridge, carrying his briefcase and jacket as if he was getting off quite normally at an airport.

Elinor Senkler sat immobile. It seemed as if everything had suddenly stopped. After the heavy noises of the impact and the groan of tearing metal, the sudden silence was erie.

Then she thought, we're alive. We've survived.

She looked left. Edmund Senkler was moving, groping with his hand under the seat, and Elinor realised, he's feeling for the camera.

"Eddie, leave it!" she screamed at him, pulling, tugging at her seat belt. "Get out, it's gonna blow!"

She felt the seat belt loosen, jumped up and rushed

into the aisle. She faltered. Which way out? Edmund brushed past, running towards the exit door a few rows away, behind their seats, and grabbed the handle that would swing it open. As he was beginning to pull, he saw fire. The wing outside was ablaze.

"No!" a stewardess yelled across at him. "This way, this way!"

Edmund started saying something about the fire.

"No!" she shouted back, shaking her head. "*This* side!"

Elinor heard the stewardess shouting and stumbled in her direction, struggling through the four-seat centre section over abandoned camera cases, bags, blankets and other items scattered across the seats and floor. She held onto the headrests to steady herself, moving as quickly as she could, and reached the far aisle. Directly ahead was the open emergency exit, and she saw the stewardess shoving passengers through it into daylight.

For a while she had lost sight of Edmund, but he was suddenly there, right behind her. He had found a different route across the cabin, through the narrow passageway between the toilet cabinets. Together again, the Senklers went through the exit door and hurried across the wing to the ground. Ahead, Elinor saw a man running away.

"It's going to blow!" she yelled, and they struggled across the mud and began running.

Hans Neeb had been helping in the forward doorway, then left the aircraft, walking, half-running down the escape chute. He looked back as he reached the ground and saw smoke and flames coming from the far side of the wreckage, and began running, because he *knew* the 747 would explode.

After a short distance he stopped and looked back again. People were still leaping down the escape chute from the door he had just left, and others were escaping down a second chute over the right wing. The rear section of the aircraft behind the wings was completely gone, and the tail seemed to have disintegrated. Towards the front section of the jumbo, there were large cracks and some damage near the ground. The far side of the aircraft was covered in flames, and thick dark smoke was rising into the sky.

A voice was calling for help. Hans Neeb turned and saw an elderly man struggling nearby. He went up to the man, got an arm around him, and walked him slowly away, taking his weight across his shoulders. When they had gone some distance, Hans Neeb lowered the man gently to the ground. He would be safe there, Neeb decided. What he really needed was an ambulance.

Explosions shook the burning jet. Neeb looked up and saw passengers still coming out, while the flames flared up fiercely. Coming towards him was the familiar face of his German colleague, Dr Gerd Kampf-Emden. His friend had no shoes and blood was dripping from one of his feet.

Hans Neeb ran over and the two men shook hands.

"*Ja*," Kampf-Emden said grimly in German, "we have just escaped from the devil's shovel."

Mother Dietlinde sat dazed in her seat. She had no idea how long she had sat there, staring ahead into the gloom. At first she was not aware of the fire, or of the danger she was in. She saw her passport and purse lying on the floor next to her feet, and she unstrapped herself and bent down to pick them up. The bag they had fallen from was overturned. She righted the bag carefully and returned the two items neatly to their places, working unhurriedly, oblivious to all that was happening around her.

When she stood up, she was astounded. She saw wreckage and destruction inside the aircraft, and felt desperately alone. There was no one else in sight. She felt dreadfully afraid. Turning towards the back of the jumbo, to where the four Solanus sisters had been sitting, all she could see was a tangled mess. She thought she saw flames. Was the jumbo on fire?

Bewildered, she tried to climb over the wreckage in the aisle next to her, praying fervently, "Lord God, if you still need me in the mission, then help me now, when I need help."

The impact had left me stunned in my seat.

"Get out!" Lynn yelled across at me. "Get out!" She was struggling with her seat belt.

I unbuckled my belt and Garett's and dragged him into the aisle. He moved without speaking, eyes wide, like a robot. I leaned over to pull up the armrests. We had to get Brendon out. The whole side of the aircraft was a sheet of flame licking up against the glass of the windows. It crackled and roared as it burned. I thought, we'll never make it. We're going to be burned.

Lynn leaped across the aisle, came up from behind and unbuckled Brendon's belt, shouting, "Wake up, it's a crash! It's a crash!" and dragged him, mumbling and half-asleep, into the aisle.

"Is he all right?"

"Yes," Lynn cried, "yes!"

In the seat behind us I saw an elderly man with blood on his forehead. He was making no effort to get up. He sat looking dazed, the blood dripping down. I did not know whether to help him or not.

"Get out!" Lynn shouted to me. "Quickly!"

But there was debris all around us. Large sections of the ceiling blocked our path, and the overhead lockers had broken off. All sorts of wreckage was raining down, white powdery material, chips of plastic, pieces of luggage. The whole aircraft seemed to be closing in on us, and all the time there were flames at the windows and a smell that tore at the throat and nostrils.

Behind us, the rear section of the 747 was missing. A diffused light filtered through the jagged wreckage and Lynn moved instinctively towards it, seeking a way out.

"No!" I shouted. "Go forward!" I had Garett's hand in mine and pushed ahead. I managed, one-handed, to hurl aside some of the fallen ceiling, and smashed a path through the wreckage in the aisle. As we headed towards the front I felt someone close behind. I looked over my shoulder and saw it was the nun.

There was no escape to the left, only flames. I saw the safety diagram in my mind: we had to go towards the front, and then to the right. Dragging Garett by the hand, I reached the kitchen and pulled him into it. From the starboard side of the aircraft a man's voice was shouting loudly and hoarsely, "*Raus!* Out! *Raus!*"

The kitchen was in ruins and some of the equipment had fallen over, blocking our path. A man came up beside me and together we kicked once, twice. The biggest object broke up in large fragments and we were through. The nun ran past.

Mother Dietlinde found herself sliding down the escape chute with her bag in her hand. Near the bottom she got stuck. She stood up, saw the muddy earth around her and felt faint. Everything went dark before her eyes and she felt she was falling.

Someone took her by the arm and she heard a man's voice say, "Quick, sister, we must get away from here."

She leaned gratefully on the man and was led away across the mud, passing through a nightmarish scene of bodies, injured people and wreckage that seemed to spread everywhere. She stumbled on, weak and dazed, and finally reached a mound in the field, where she stopped and bowed her head, deeply shocked.

I could see the open doorway ahead, daylight streaming in, and people leaping out and down. At that moment I lost sight of Lynn. I looked back desperately, but could not see her. Oh no, no, no, I thought, hesitating near the doorway, flanked by two yelling crew members, what's happened to them? I did not know what to do. Should I throw Garett down the chute and go back for them? Should we jump together and leave them? Or should we both go back?

"Lynn," I shouted. "Where are you?"

There was no response. The two crew members near the door were grabbing me and shouting.

I did not know, because I could not see, that Brendon had broken free from Lynn's grip. He ran towards the first-class section, where the impact had opened up cracks so large that passengers had fallen through, still strapped to their seats. Lynn chased after Brendon, reached out and grabbed him before he disappeared.

"Lynn," I yelled again from the exit, unwilling to leave.

Suddenly she was coming through the wreckage. She had Brendon by the hand.

"Get out," she shouted as she came. "We're all right. Get out!"

The dark-haired steward had me by the arm, and shoved my shoulder, shouting, "*Raus! Raus!*" He hurled me through the door. I landed on the chute and scrambled down. Alongside me was Garett, shoved by a stewardess. And behind came Lynn with Brendon, both in their socks.

There was an explosion as we reached the ground, a hollow boom from the far side of the aircraft. A man shouted, "Run, it's going to explode! Run!"

We got up and ran. I was terrified that the fuel tanks would ignite and engulf us in a giant explosion. Ahead, a man with a limp was running wildly across the bush, looking back, stumbling, regaining his balance, and carrying on. Brendon had no shoes. I picked him up and ran with him over the rough ground. He seemed dazed, half-asleep. When we had gone about fifty yards Garett tripped and fell face down. He scrambled to his feet, his face covered in mud. My wife was crying, "My babies, oh, my babies! Thank God, you're safe. Thank God."

Back at the doorway, stragglers were still arriving. A woman slipped coming through from the kitchen and fell heavily. Stewardess Evelyn Rehm leaned down to help, lost her balance and tumbled through the doorway onto the chute, and landed in a heap on the ground. Above her, Tom Scott went on pushing people out. The jumbo was shaking beneath him, smoke filled the interior, and flames were shooting up fiercely on the port side.

And then came the moment when no more passengers appeared.

Tom Scott stood alone in the doorway and knew that all those who could walk were out. It's a time bomb, he thought, and it's going to explode at any second. He wanted to jump out himself and run, to get as far away as he could, before the big explosion ripped everything apart.

But he knew, too, that he couldn't leave without making a final check to see if there was anyone still aboard who might be trapped, unconscious, or unable to walk.

Tom Scott ran forward, looking left and right in the quiet compartment. He saw nobody. He turned back to take a last look in the non-smoking section between the wings, hoping anxiously that it would be empty.

The jumbo was quivering. There were small

explosions off to the left, and he wanted to get out of it right away. One last look and he could flee with a clear conscience. He peered through the dust and smoke . . . and felt an icy hand clutch at his heart.

Someone was still·in the burning aircraft.

An elderly man was sitting way back on the port side of the non-smoking area. He was leaned over in his seat, blood dripping from a wound in his forehead.

Oh no, Tom despaired, oh no. A conflict raged in his mind: if I try to save him, I'll never make it. He must weigh about 200 pounds. I'll never be able to get him out of here in time and, heck, he's an old man, he's probably not going to be around for much longer anyway. I've risked my life long enough in here, I should get out. I have a duty to my wife and parents.

These thoughts, terrible thoughts, flashed through his mind, but he knew even as he was thinking them that he would *have to* try to save the old man. He couldn't leave him. If he did, it would haunt him for the rest of his life.

Tom Scott pushed through the wrecked interior and gripped the old man's shoulder. The man looked up, startled, and asked the steward in German, "Where is my case?"

"Forget your case, grandpa," Tom Scott yelled at him. "We've got to get out of here."

Tom reached down and dragged him into the aisle. The flames were right up against the windows and the burning fuel was hissing and crackling. There was an ominous vibration. The aircraft was about to explode. Tom Scott had his arm around the old man's body and was half-dragging him through the wreckage. Faster, faster! They didn't have much time.

Tom got him to the door, bent down and took the man's weight over his shoulders. They went down the escape chute together and ran clumsily through the mud towards the other passengers they could see gathered about a hundred yards away.

When they reached the people Tom Scott noticed the old man was clutching a dark attache case. He had saved it after all.

Margaret Hooker was not sure if she had been unconscious or if she had simply been sitting, numbed, in her seat down in the baggage hold all the time. She was surrounded by metal, and could not remember clearly what had happened. There was a board in front of her and she managed to place it: the board had been in the first class compartment, a yard or two in front of her, before the take-off began. The stewardesses had used it to hold trays and drinks while they were serving.

Right by her shoulder the fuselage had burst open. Through a jagged hole she could see small flames on the ground outside and a man was running towards the aircraft, leaping over rings of fire. He must have seen her, but he said nothing, and she eventually lost sight of him.

She loosened her seat belt, but discovered she could not move. Her foot was caught in the wreckage. She felt no pain and there was no blood, so why couldn't she get her foot out?

She tensed herself, in case it hurt, and jerked her leg really hard, and tore her foot free from whatever was holding it down. When she examined it, she saw there was a deep, ragged gash right through her foot, from top to bottom. But still no blood appeared, and she could not feel a thing.

She tried to stand up, but something kept pulling her back. Puzzled, Margaret looked down. Her trousers were snagged on the bottom of the seat. She tugged at them, hoping they would tear free, but they would not. She was trapped in the aircraft.

There was only one thing to do. Margaret wriggled out of her trousers, thankful for the elasticated top, and stepped through the hole in the fuselage in her underwear. She was standing on the ground, surrounded by jet fuel, with fires burning only a short distance away, and felt the coldness of the fuel on her bare feet. But she did not feel afraid and believed she was thinking very clearly. She reached back into the wreckage, unhooked her trousers and calmly put them on again.

Looking through the crack from outside, Margaret

saw the rows of seats hanging about knee-high off the ground. And then she saw her new friend Carol Mall lying sprawled back in her seat, with her eyes closed and blood oozing from cuts on her eyebrows. Carol opened her eyes.

"My God, Carol," Margaret cried out, "what has happened?"

Carol did not reply. She lay staring soundlessly up at her companion, and Margaret guessed that Carol had been seriously injured.

"Don't worry," Margaret reassured her, leaning in. "I won't leave you." She reached across and unfastened Carol's seat belt. Carol raised her arms, but she still did not speak.

"I'll get you out of here, Carol, don't you worry."

Margaret slipped her arms under Carol's body and lifted her up, surprised by how little she weighed and how easy she was to move. Talking softly, Margaret moved Carol slowly through the torn metal and out of the crack. As she was doing this, Margaret noticed her handbag lying right there on the seat, with her passport and money and personal items all spilled out. She thought instinctively, grab your passport, it's a valuable document, you'll need it.

She scooped it up in one hand, dropped it back in the handbag, swung the bag over her arm and set off, bent under Carol Mall's weight, stepping slowly through the puddles of fuel next to the fuselage.

Margaret became aware of other things: dark, oily smoke rising into the sky from somewhere behind her, and voices from the first class compartment calling for help. But there was nothing she could do for them. She staggered on past the nose and saw people standing some distance away.

"Hurry," someone shouted to her. "It's going to explode!"

She could not move any faster. She struggled on alone, until some of the people from the group ran over and took Carol from her arms. They all ran together after that, away from the burning jet. They were not far away when *Hessen* exploded, the fire roaring into the sky above the cabin she and Carol had just left, and Margaret thought, my God, all those people are still inside.

But no one could get near. The flames were too fierce.

I looked back and saw flames erupting high over the cabin. A dark cloud of smoke swirled into the sky. Dust and oily fluff was floating down on us. The tail section was missing and the nose had been damaged, and people were running away. While I was running, I noticed with some surprise that the shattered jet had swivelled round and now lay facing back the way we had come. I called to Lynn, "The jet spun right round, do you see that? We turned right round!"

Lynn did not understand, and sobbed out, "What?"

We ran on. I was shouting, "Keep going, keep going!" afraid parts of the 747 might fly off. When we reached the top of a slope, the skyline seemed to come alive. A crowd of Kenyans came rushing towards the aircraft. Four of them, a woman and three men, came up and embraced us, and held our hands.

"You are safe," the woman said, wide-eyed, and stroked the children. "God is with you today!"

In the embrace of strangers, I felt an overwhelming sense of comfort, like being a child again, being mothered and protected. After all the travelling, the death and sudden destruction, we had come back to warmth and compassion in the arms of Africa.

A man offered us his broken shoes, pointing at the mud-covered socks on Lynn's and Brendon's feet. I looked at the man and felt close to tears.

8 • *Trapped*

Hessen's **impact** with the earth caused massive destruction in the first class compartment. Jagged cracks opened up in the floor, so deep they went all the way through to the ground, and the passenger cabin began breaking up. The floor sloped at different angles, seats were torn off and sections of the staircase and the upstairs lounge broke loose, crashing down onto passengers on the main deck below.

Purser Heide Tischer, aged thirty-nine, and stewardess Lydia Lux, twenty-five, were sitting strapped into a twin-seat on the port side, directly under the lounge, when it came down. At almost the same time, the cabin floor beneath them collapsed. They gripped hands, Heide Tischer cried out, "My God!" and Lydia Lux screamed.

As the 747's long slide across the Kenyan bush ended Captain Krack reached out and pulled the four engine fire switches. He and Flight Engineer

Hahn sprang onto the cockpit seats and reached for the overhead escape hatch. It would not open. They pushed and hammered at it with their bare hands, but still nothing happened. It was stuck tight.

Flight Engineer Hahn thought, "Try the service hatch door." He jumped down and operated the lock on the door, situated on the right-hand side of the cockpit. He managed to open it and wrenched the door inwards. It swung in about five inches, then jammed. Rudi Hahn pulled at it with both hands, but the impact must have damaged the floor. The door would not open any further. He could stick an arm or a leg out, but that was all.

Co-pilot Schacke saw Krack and Hahn struggling with the jammed cockpit escape exits, and realised that their only way out now would be through the cocktail bar and lounge, and then down the stairs to the first class compartment. He pushed through to the top of the stairs, and hesitated. The stairway was blocked by wreckage.

Captain Krack and Rudi Hahn joined him, and together they prodded at the wreckage and saw it give. The whole thing might shatter under their weight.

"We'll *have* to go down there," co-pilot Schacke said unhappily.

Rudi Hahn jumped. The wrecked staircase broke and he fell right through it, landing heavily on his back on the cabin floor below. He sat up and got to his feet, clutching his right shoulder, his face twisted in agony. He could barely move his arm.

Captain Krack came crashing down next to Hahn, and more debris tumbled with him. The commander recovered quickly and began shouting, "*Raus*! Out! Everybody out!"

Krack saw a large gap in the main deck floor, jumped down into it and scrambled his way out through a hole in the starboard side of the fuselage. Hahn followed behind Krack, but decided to head left instead, and crawled out of the aircraft through a crack in the port side.

Hahn got to his feet and was stumbling off awkwardly, holding his injured shoulder, when two men came running across the bush, and led him away to safety. Later medical staff told him he had dislocated his shoulder.

In the ruins below the first class compartment, cabin crew members Heide Tischer and Lydia Lux found themselves trapped in a metal cavern. There was a narrow gap in front of Heide's right foot that widened out, becoming a sizeable opening in the fuselage. Through it, she could see daylight and the fields outside.

Heide freed herself from her seat and squeezed through the gap, tearing her clothes as she went. Lydia Lux followed and they stepped through the opening in the side of the aircraft and found themselves standing outside, but confronted by a wall of flames.

Heide noticed a patch of ground to her right where the fire had not yet taken hold, and the two women used this as an escape route, running between the flames and the wrecked fuselage. They ran past the 747's nose to the starboard side, which was still relatively unaffected by fire, and began helping injured passengers.

In row 1 of the first class compartment, right up in the nose of the aircraft, Bob Laburn emerged slowly from his daze. Screams and cries were coming from somewhere behind him and he could hear a voice calling out, "*Raus! Raus!*"

He struggled to breathe, gulping for air, still strapped to his seat. I must have hit my chest on my knees, he thought, and tried to straighten himself, but couldn't. Pain went shooting up his spine to his neck, and he realised that something serious had happened to his back.

Where are my glasses, he wondered, feeling around blindly with his hands. I was wearing them a moment ago. They *must* be here somewhere.

As he was searching, the man who had been sitting silently in the twin-seat next to him jumped up suddenly and dashed towards the back of the jumbo. Bob Laburn peered after him and realised with a growing sense of urgency that he had to get out of the aircraft as soon as he could.

He unfastened his seat belt and staggered to his feet. Standing up made little difference; he still felt unable to breathe properly and leaned on the seat in agony, staring at his surroundings. He noticed something strange. Despite the immense shock of the impact, the airline's complimentary red roses for first class passengers were still attached to seats all over the cabin. Another thing he noticed was that the woman in the seat directly behind him was not moving. But there was little that Bob Laburn could do to help her. He could barely walk.

He moved away slowly and painfully in a stooped, huddled-up posture, shuffling along the debris-strewn aisle. The floor was tilted down and ended in a large uneven hole at the point where the staircase from the cockpit and the upper-deck cocktail lounge joined the main passenger deck. Down in the hole a fire had broken out, and Bob Laburn saw flames leaping up about knee-high.

At almost the same moment he noticed a possible way out: from the hole, there was a rough pathway through the under-floor wreckage, and it led directly to a crack in the side of the fuselage.

Bob Laburn made a quick decision. He shuffled to the edge of the hole, and jumped. He dropped about ten feet into the flames and landed on something soft, but the pain in his back was unbelievable. Debris was burning fiercely all around him: linings, upholstery and fittings.

He pushed ahead through the flames as quickly as he could, aiming for the crack in the fuselage. The crack was close to the ground, and he was able to get through it relatively easily and stagger away through the mud in front of the starboard wing. Surprisingly, despite passing through fire, his clothes had not caught alight.

The urge to get away from the aircraft before it exploded kept him going. But moving was difficult and painful and, after about fifty yards, he slumped down next to a large stone, feeling exhausted.

Helmut Frankenberg, forty-four-year-old partner in the Penaten Creme business at Rhoendorf on the Rhine, and his wife Christel were trapped in their seats on the port side of the first class compartment. The floor had opened up beneath them, and the ceiling and parts of the cocktail lounge had fallen down. They were squeezed between rows of seats in the dark, and barely able to see what was happening.

Footsteps sounded above their heads, but nobody came. Was it the crew? Christel Frankenberg called out again and again.

Her husband was sprawled back next to her, unable to move. He felt something wet and shouted, "There's kerosene running over us!"

Christel struggled frantically. She twisted her body, trying to free her feet and legs. Her husband spoke quietly, saying, "Don't panic. Just keep calm. We can only pray that it's all over quickly."

But Christel went on struggling and eventually broke free. She pushed herself backwards out of a crack in the side of the aircraft and fell to the burning ground outside. She looked back through the hole at her husband, but he did not speak. He seemed to be unconscious, and she did not know how to help him.

A man ran through the flames and grabbed hold of her, shouting, "It's going to explode!" He dragged her away as explosions shook the wreck and they ran together through the smoke and flying metal.

Alarmed by Rudi Hahn's fall through the wrecked stairs, co-pilot Schacke ran back to the cockpit. In desperation, he decided to try the jammed overhead hatch once more. He jumped onto the seat, stretched his hands above his head, and shoved hard against it.

For a moment nothing happened. Then, to his surprise, the hatch opened.

Relieved, Schacke looked out of it and down the port side of the jumbo. He saw flames darting up on the ground below and fire on the left wing. From up there, the flames seemed to encircle *Hessen*'s nose and he thought, no, not this exit, try the other side.

He jumped off the seat and stepped across the cockpit to the jammed service door on the starboard side and tried to prise it open. But it was no use. He couldn't get it to move. Something was holding it back. He would have to go through the overhead hatch after all.

He climbed back onto the seat. Grabbing one of the emergency handles, he heaved himself up and through the hatch. For a moment he clung to the roof of the cockpit and the whole scene was spread vividly below him. There were small fires all around and the ground was covered with jet fuel. He could see several cracks forward of the wing where the fuselage had burst open.

Schacke dropped, using his legs and the steel cord of the emergency escape reel to lower himself down the steep side of the jumbo to the ground. As he landed, he heard a voice shouting for help. It came from one of the cracks in the fuselage, and he ran to see what he could do.

As he reached the crack, a woman stepped out, hysterical, her clothes torn. Schacke put a hand on her shoulder and urged her quickly away in the direction of the other survivors he could see standing some distance away.

Schacke turned back and, through a crack in the fuselage, saw Captain Krack inside the 747, helping a couple trapped in their seats, a few yards from the burning wing.

The captain had re-entered the burning 747 through stewardess Evelyn Rehm's door, directly in front of the starboard wing, after first crawling out of a hole in the fuselage. Somehow, he had managed to climb up the escape chute between the fleeing passengers and set about trying to free some of the trapped survivors.

Before Schacke could reach Captain Krack, an injured woman covered in blood staggered from the wreckage and collapsed. The co-pilot ran to help, and tried to drag her away.

He was standing deep in fuel and felt sick and weak from the fumes. He tripped over something and fell, hitting the side of his head. Blood was dripping from his ear onto his uniform, but he got back to his feet, picked the woman up and managed to drag her clear.

Hearing cries coming from the forward section, Schacke hurried back, but as he approached, explosions ripped through the wrecked aircraft and flames flared up over the cabin. The co-pilot could not get any closer. All he could do was watch.

Three rows ahead of the Frankenbergs, Malcolm Solts raised his head. He was covered in debris and dust. The seat to which he was strapped was leaning over at an angle, the left side lower than the right. Malcolm looked around in the gloom, trying to see what was left of the 747. He could not see very much.

All kinds of wreckage blocked his view.

When he looked to his left, he realised with a shock that he was almost outside the cabin. The empty seat joined to his had been flung through the metal side of the aircraft. There was a gaping crack right next to him and he could see the ground outside and small fires springing up. The twinned seats hung there, half-in, half-out, part of a heap of wreckage that rested against the muddy field.

Malcolm Solts pushed aside the debris covering him, unfastened his seat belt and stood up. He squeezed himself through a hole in the fuselage and dropped to the ground. As he landed, he saw fire creeping forward from one of the smashed engines and began running. He had gone about five or six paces when he heard a man's voice pleading, "Help! Help me out!"

Faltering, Malcolm Solts looked back. The voice called again.

Malcolm knew who it was. It was the man who had sat behind him, the man from Düsseldorf, who had spent the night talking to him up in the cocktail lounge during the flight from Frankfurt. Malcolm turned back.

There were explosions as Malcolm crawled in through the cracked fuselage, and a sheet of flame shot up. His friend of the night before was covered in wreckage, a huge metal section trapping his legs. Malcolm tried to lift it, but the metal could not be moved. He put his hands under the German's arms and tried to drag him out, but it was impossible. The man's legs were too tightly wedged.

"Leave me," the man shouted at him. "Get out!"

The fire was right next to them, the flames increasing in ferocity. Malcolm Solts did not know what to do. The man was trapped, and he couldn't get him out. But how could he simply leave him?

"Get out." The German was pushing him away.

Malcolm stumbled backwards. He saw fire everywhere. If he stayed, he would die. He jumped out of the hole he had escaped from minutes before, ducked his head and ran for his life. There were flames spreading across the field outside, climbing high over the cabin, and thick dark smoke was spiralling out of cracks and holes and broken windows. There were more explosions as he ran, and he heard the flames crackling behind him. Voices were shouting to him to get away.

Sick with fear and horror, he ran out of the smoke. Ahead, he saw a small group of people standing in the field, their eyes wide, mouths hanging, some sobbing. He went and stood with them.

On the slope, nobody spoke. They simply stood and stared, weeping, as fire engulfed the aircraft with people still on board. Christel Frankenberg was standing near the others when the big explosion came. Flames spurted up, wrapping the cabin in fire, and she knew she would never see her husband again.

9 • *The crash site*

Shortly before eight that morning, Gino Iannibelli and two of his work colleagues were standing outside the Italian Sogene Construction Company offices, about half a mile from the Nairobi runway. They were lounging in the fresh morning air, warming themselves in the brightening sunshine, while gazing idly across the grassy expanse of the airport.

An aircraft was racing down the runway, a 747 jumbo with a black nose and blue and yellow tail, the name Lufthansa standing out clearly on the white-painted body forward of the wing. They heard the roar of the engines as it gained speed and waited for the moment when it would thrust itself up from the ground and climb into the sky.

To Gino, it seemed that the aircraft was taking an awfully long time to build up speed. He had the impression that it was almost at the end of the runway. At that moment, the aircraft lifted, but it hardly climbed at all, and it was still so close to the ground. Then it began to fall.

The men shouted in horror. The 747 went on dropping steadily. The men began running to their Land Rovers without taking their eyes off the terrible sight. Still the jet sank, the tail way down and almost dragging on the ground. It was heading directly for an embanked road that crossed the line of the runway, more than half a mile out in the bush.

There was a heavy thud and a flash of flame as the left wing and engines smashed into the embanked earthwork. Gino stood watching in shock as the jumbo broke apart. Then he raced to his Land Rover with the others, jumped in and went speeding along the road.

John Kingsley-Heath, who owned safari companies in both Kenya and Botswana, should have been on the flight. But late the previous afternoon he had changed his mind.

For him, catching the Lufthansa jumbo meant getting up at five-thirty or six on the Wednesday morning at the latest, a fairly early start, so he had asked his secretary to see if she could switch his ticket to the British Airways flight that left Nairobi at about nine that morning. It hadn't been easy, but she had managed it.

"It was a bit of a rush," she told him when he called in at his office, "but I suppose if it gives you an extra hour's sleep it's all in a good cause."

They laughed about it, and he took the ticket. He had no premonitions, no uneasy feelings, but she had probably just saved his life.

Check-in time for the British Airways flight was eight o' clock and shortly before eight, Kingsley-Heath was driving swiftly along the airport road, parallel to the runway, in his Toyota station wagon. He glanced to his right and saw the Lufthansa 747 he should have been on lifting off the runway. He kept watching, his hands gripping the wheel, the vehicle almost aiming itself. He was a commercial pilot with 6,000 hours of flying experience, and he sensed that something was wrong.

My God, he thought, the bloody thing's going to stall. I can't believe it's going to get off the ground.

The Toyota almost collided with an oncoming vehicle. He had wandered into the centre of the road, and swerved back wildly, braked and pulled over to the side. When he looked again at the 747, he realised that it would crash.

Kingsley-Heath could hear the aircraft vibrating, making a strange chuh-chuh-chuh noise as it struggled on, dropping gradually lower, the nose still aimed up. He was staring at it side-on, but was unable to see if the undercarriage was extended or retracted. He jumped out of his vehicle and climbed on top of the bonnet to get a better view, and he was standing up there when the 747 went in.

At the last moment, the engines seemed to die away, as if they had been switched off. There was a tremendous sound as it impacted, and a cloud of grass and loose sand flew up. The 747 seemed to shoot forward over the road.

Kingsley-Heath jumped off the Toyota, got back inside, slammed it into gear and roared off up a dirt track in the direction of the crash. The station wagon bounced over the rough ground. He could see burning wreckage ahead.

The Toyota was the first vehicle on the scene. Kingsley-Heath drew up about two hundred yards from the aircraft, worried that the wreckage might explode and hurl fire everywhere. He jumped out and began running. The size of the aircraft and the extent of the wreckage appalled him, and he faltered, wondering suddenly what he would be able to do.

And then he saw the first survivors.

They were wandering around the burning wreckage, dazed and bewildered, their clothing torn and muddied. Nearby lay about twenty contorted bodies, many of them charred and burned. Kingsley-Heath went forward to see how he could help, and noticed people streaming towards the crash site from all directions, some running from the airport, and others coming up from the main road. He looked at the long groove scraped in the ground by the jumbo's belly and saw debris, suitcases and wrecked luggage strewn across the bush. Some people in the approaching crowd were stooping to pick up items as they they got nearer. The looting enraged Kingsley-Heath. He thought irrationally, if I had my gun with me, I'd probably shoot them.

Gino Iannibelli and his two colleagues arrived at the crash site in minutes. They turned their Land Rovers off the road and drove across the bush, stopped, jumped down and ran to the wreck.

It was a terrible scene. Bodies, pieces of metal and shredded luggage were spread everywhere. In the middle of it all lay what was left of the jumbo: the "head" of the aircraft, with thick black smoke bursting out of it, and fire spreading rapidly along the left wing.

The three Italians ran in, put their arms around a group of stumbling and wounded survivors and dragged them away from the flames as something exploded. They returned to the aircraft again and again, picking up those who could not walk and carrying them to safety. Those who were unconscious they laid at the side of the embanked road to await the ambulances they could hear screaming in the distance. How many of these, Gino thought in despair, are already dead?

A short distance from the wreck he found a blonde-haired little girl, not much older than three, wearing a red suit. She was lying motionless, her small head turned to one side on the ground. As he looked at her everything broke inside him. He began to weep.

"Come here," he shouted to his friends.

One of them came over, knelt down and felt for the little girl's pulse. For a moment the man held the tiny wrist in his hand, then placed it gently back at her side. He looked at Gino.

"She is dead," he said quietly.

Gino turned away and wiped his eyes. He felt his courage going. It was too much for a soul to bear. He began walking back to his vehicle, his eyes burning.

Among the hundreds of people running to the scene was press photographer Samuel Ouma, of the Nairobi *Daily Nation*. He had been at the airport to photograph the West German Bundestag members after their arrival from Frankfurt aboard the Lufthansa 747.

Once the pictures were taken and the Bundestag team were on their way in to the city, Samuel Ouma slung his camera over his shoulder and went over to the airport bar for an early morning beer. He had been there only a few minutes when he heard people screaming, and someone shouted, "The jumbo has crashed!"

People were running from the building and Samuel Ouma ran after them, leaving his unfinished beer on the bar. He headed for the runway, looked about and saw a dense black column of smoke rising into the sky near the Mombasa road.

He took pictures as he ran, using his telephoto lens to bring the horrible scene closer: the jet lying belly-down and keeled over in the mud, the nose aiming back the way it had been travelling, flames flaring up fiercely from the portside wing, and dark clouds of billowing, swirling smoke.

By now, hundreds of people were heading for the embanked earth road. Ahead, Samuel could see a trail of wreckage and bodies, and as he focused his camera he heard voices crying out for help. But there were others already helping. Rescuers were dashing into the torn metal and dragging people out, and he kept shooting picture after picture. The photographs seemed to compose themselves: twisted wreckage, shocked faces of survivors, curling smoke, the grotesque poses of the dead.

Later these appalling sights would be flashed around the world. By nightfall, the horror he had seen through his lens would be shared with millions as newspapers splashed his photographs across their front pages and television networks beamed them into the homes of people in countries he had never seen.

But Samuel Ouma did not think about that while he was shooting. Shocked by the scenes around him, he felt ill. It was the sort of thing you read about in books or saw in the cinema. He had never expected to see it in real life, on a peaceful morning that had seemed to begin like so many others.

A short distance away from the wreck, a small group of survivors gathered on a slope, examining each other for injuries. John Bing looked up in amazement as Terry Partridge walked over, carrying his briefcase.

"It fell into my lap when we crashed," Terry explained.

As he watched the jumbo burning, Terry noticed, for the first time, that the back half of the aircraft was missing, and realised that the crash had been far worse than he thought. Some people must have been killed. And it shocked him to think he could have been one of them.

A man's voice called out for help. He was lying on the ground near the wrecked aircraft, clutching his back. The Bings and Terry Partridge and some of the others ran down the slope to see what they could do.

"My back," the man said. "I can't move my back."

Terry looked at him and thought, he might have broken it. We shouldn't try to move him.

Jean Bing, who was a radiographer, echoed his thoughts. "He should stay lying down until the ambulance comes," she said. "He shouldn't be moved."

But after some discussion, the survivors agreed to move the man away from the wreck, in case there were more explosions.

Terry Partridge rolled up his jacket, dropped to his knees and gently placed it under the man's head while the others, including a Lufthansa steward, searched for a board or something to carry him on. A fibreglass sheet was found in the wreckage and they got the wounded man onto it and carried him carefully away.

A Land Rover drew up and the driver jumped down and shouted, "Put him in the back. I'll take him to the hospital."

They loaded the injured man into the vehicle and someone climbed in next to him. The small group watched the Land Rover move off slowly across the uneven ground. No one spoke. Feeling confused, lost and shocked, they wandered towards the embanked earth road that was now crowded with onlookers.

Gino Iannibelli met some of the group as he was heading back to his vehicle. He saw a middle-aged couple and a young man stumbling unsteadily through the wreckage. The woman had lost a shoe and was having difficulty walking over the tufted grass, and the man, probably her husband, had lost his jacket. The younger man had all his clothes and carried a briefcase. To Gino, they seemed dazed and deeply shocked, and moved quite strangely.

He could not speak English, so Gino pointed up the slope and mimed the question, "Do you want something warm to drink?" He led them to his Land Rover, helped them in, and drove along the embanked road to the Sogene Construction Company's staff canteen. One of the firm's English consultants came to help, sat them down and made them a cup of tea.

"I was in the D-Day landings in Normandy," the consultant said, shaking his head, "but seeing that plane come down was worse than anything that happened there."

Back at the crash site, Hermann Hennecke was stumbling about the bush. He heard voices and made out six people approaching.

"Could you please help me to the airport," he called out. "I've lost my glasses and I can't see very well."

The six survivors came over to join him, but stood without speaking, watching the flames shooting up from the jumbo. In the distance they could hear sirens shrieking, but none of them reacted. It was as if they were outsiders and had never been on *Hessen* at all.

After a while the group began walking towards the embanked earth road in the distance. At the road one of the survivors stopped a car and asked the driver to take them back to the airport.

"Get in," he urged and opened the doors.

Hermann Hennecke and the other six got in and sat tightly together as the car began to edge away through the crowds. Hennecke turned to take one last look at *Hessen*. For the first time, he felt an overwhelming sense of gratitude.

Bob Laburn, his shoes thick with clay, lay on the ground, resting on his left elbow, trying to find a position that would ease the pain in his back and neck. Nothing seemed to help. Any slight movement brought agony.

A figure approached and sat down on Bob Laburn's stone. Laburn looked up. He saw a man with blood running from a gash in his right cheek, recognised him, and called out, "Hello, John. Fancy meeting you here."

The newcomer was John Hall, general manager of Southern Cross Steel, in Johannesburg, who had met him many times before on business. The two men were unaware that they had been on the same flight until they found each other in a strange field, thousands of miles from home, in torn and blood-stained clothing, with a blazing aircraft for a backdrop. It was a bizarre setting.

"Are you badly hurt?"

"No, I'm all right," John Hall touched his cheek, "except for this. But it's not serious."

John had escaped down an emergency chute on the starboard side. Sitting directly behind him in the economy class cabin had been his managing director and business colleague, Anthony Grant, and he had not seen him since the aircraft had gone down.

A Land Rover was moving slowly through the wreckage and Bob Laburn saw some men picking up survivors and helping the injured. One of the men came over and tried to lift him into the Land Rover, but another survivor intervened.

"Leave him until an ambulance comes," Herbert Frosch told them. "He's injured his back. We should be careful how we move him."

Bob Laburn remained half-lying in the centre of the small group of people, gritting his teeth against the pain.

Survivors were still running away from the wreck, but as they did so, hundreds of curious people passed them, hurrying the other way, some running right in among the injured. Some of these people went to help, dragging and carrying survivors out on their backs; but others went to loot, snatching often worthless items from the debris.

When the 747 crashed, West German diplomatic courier Knut Müller was travelling south to Pretoria with a sealed diplomatic bag. He jumped from the wrecked jumbo after it came to rest and ran for his life. A blast caught him, lifting him off his feet, and he blacked out.

When he came to, he was lying in mud, close to the wrecked jumbo, unable to move because of the pain of his injuries. A man was standing over him. The man took his tie and tried to pull the shoes from his feet.

Knut Müller cried out for help. A fellow survivor ran back and the looter fled, clutching the tie. Knut never saw it again, or the diplomatic bag he had been carrying. German officials spent the next few days searching the accident site, probing the ground with steel rods and sifting through the burned-out wreckage for the secret coding machine the bag contained. They found no sign of it.

Another who had a similar experience was Captain Heinz Peper, from Busdorf, in Schleswig. On his way to Durban to take command of the container ship *Pallas*, he was knocked flat by an explosion as he was fleeing the burning 747. He regained consciousness, to find himself lying on the ground. Looters were searching through the pockets of the dead and injured near him, taking passports, wallets, travellers cheques, watches, rings and money.

Too shocked to speak or cry out, the captain watched the looters coming towards him and felt hands feeling in his pockets. They took everything he had, even his captain's card.

We stood, weepy and shaken, four people on a slight

rise in the muddy field, looking back at the wreck. Sirens were screaming in the distance, and the flames were right over the cabin where we had been sitting. I thought of the blood-smeared old man we had left in the seat behind us, and felt sick with anguish.

"All those poor people," Lynn was crying. "Those poor people."

We had not seen more than eight other survivors. Where were all the rest? Were we the only ones who had got out? It was so difficult to believe what was happening. At that moment we should have been sitting comfortably in our seats, thousands of feet in the sky, flying towards Johannesburg. But here we were, in a field we had never seen before, and all we had were our lives. Everything else was going up in smoke: our clothes, passports, money, papers and cameras.

"I knew it, I knew it," Lynn cried.

We held each other and the children and I thought, we were so close to dying, so close. But we made it. A few rows further back and we wouldn't be standing here. Why had *we* been saved?

Then a group of what were obviously survivors staggered up, a man and two women and, not far behind them, another two women. It was a relief to see them. We could hear they were Americans from their accents.

The three in front, we found out later, were Karl,

Renate and Nancy Kahn, and the two women helping each other along were the sisters Tillie Harmel and Gladys Golman, all struggling together through the rough African bush. The earth was caked onto them, their eyes were wide and their faces taut. Tillie Harmel carried a shoe in one hand and was breathing harshly, her mouth wide open, and clutching her side.

"Are you all right?" I called out, but no one answered the question.

They stopped and looked back.

"Where are all the people?" Renate Kahn asked. "Surely we can't be the only ones who got out."

We stared down the slope, but all we could see were crowds of onlookers and, beyond them, the wreck.

"There must be others somewhere."

I heard a rumbling noise and saw a grey Land Rover coming across the bush. It drew up next to us and a man leaned from the driver's window and shouted, "Are any of you hurt?"

"We're all right," one of the Americans called out. "Just a little shaken up."

"Have you got a cigarette?" Nancy Kahn asked. "Please, I must have a cigarette." She felt shocked and shaky, and needed one badly.

A cigarette was passed through the window and the man leaned out to light it for her. Nancy inhaled deeply, eyes closed, as if her whole being was centred on that cigarette. She had never known such craving.

"Climb in," the man said. "I'll take you all back to the airport."

"Don't worry about us," someone in the group said. "We'll be all right. Why don't you see if you can help those people down at the plane?"

The Land Rover moved off down the slope. At that moment the airport fire engines finally reached the crash site and came swerving through the people, sirens blaring, and closed in on the burning wreck.

The heat kept the firemen back, but they got two tenders in close to the burning port wing, and another two in front of the nose, and sprayed foam into the flames. Nearby stood a rescue vehicle with cutting equipment, but there was little those men could do.

From the slope, we could see the foam jetting out in arcs, and the crowds of onlookers surrounding the aircraft. The flames had been sucked into the cockpit and dense black smoke streamed out of the open crew escape hatch in the roof. The jet was now a tube of fire; the firemen were too late.

A few minutes behind the fire brigade came the ambulances, and the fight to save the injured began.

Malcolm Solts went limping across to join the survivors gathered ahead of *Hessen*'s blunted nose, not far from the embanked road. His legs were cut and badly bruised, and there was something wrong with his right knee. Each time he bent it, pain stabbed his leg.

The survivors appeared bewildered and had blank stares. No one was speaking. The only noise was the crackling of flames and explosions coming from the 747.

Looters were darting through the wreckage, picking up items, sometimes passing right by the struggling survivors. Suddenly, a ragged line of uniformed men armed with clubs and automatic weapons appeared. These were members of the military General Service Unit, which had a camp in the area.

As Malcolm Solts watched, the brown-shirted soldiers fired into the air and charged. There was a scramble to get away. Looters went sprawling in the mud and others ran over them. They ran wildly up the slope, giving shrill cries, as the soldiers moved in behind them.

The chase did not last long. About thirty yards from the wreck, the Unit halted and cordoned off the area.

One person who did not see the looters or the arrival of the soldiers was Carol Mall. The American woman from the Agency for International Development in Addis Ababa lay on her back, gravely injured and barely conscious, in the centre of a huddle of people.

Near Carol sat her friend and fellow passenger Margaret Hooker, who had promised, "We'll get you out, Carol. We'll get you out."

Margaret was nursing her gashed foot and watching as the men who had helped carry Carol from the wreck tried to make her comfortable on the ground. One of them tried to raise her head so they could slide a handbag under it. But Carol cried out in pain. Her reaction startled them, and they decided to leave her lying as she was. No one realised then that Carol had broken her neck.

Margaret was distracted by a Lufthansa stewardess pointing at her arm. She looked down and saw she had a deep cut near the elbow, and the flesh was hanging open. Surprisingly, there was very little blood, and she could not feel a thing. The stewardess passed her an airline scarf and she bound the wound together, knotting the ends of the material.

Next to Margaret Hooker sat the uniformed man she had seen running past while she was still trapped in the jumbo's baggage hold. He was trying to cheer everyone up.

"I bet you could do with a cup of tea," he said to her.

"Never mind the cup of tea," Margaret told him. "I could do with a drink!"

The man laughed and a few of the others smiled.

An ambulance drove up and a group of people who had been helping at the wreck ran up, carrying a young child dressed in a jumper suit. The child was unconscious, and they placed her gently in the back of the ambulance.

A doctor, who had arrived in the ambulance along with several first aid workers, examined Carol Mall. He tugged at her sweater, to pull it away from the upper arm so he could give her an injection, but the action tightened the sweater against her neck. She groaned out loud and the doctor quickly let go and rolled up her sleeve instead.

The helpers had brought a stretcher and they moved Carol carefully onto it and placed her in the ambulance. Margaret Hooker climbed into the back, sat down and braced herself as the vehicle began to move, siren wailing, over the rough ground towards the road crowded with sightseers' cars.

Wandering across the bush, Edmund and Elinor Senkler headed for the embanked road in the distance. Elinor picked up a piece of metal about the size of a chocolate bar and ran her hands over its smooth surface.

"We're alive! A miracle!" she repeated again and again as they walked. They had come out of the crash with hardly a scratch. She carried the piece of metal a few paces before dropping it.

The Senklers passed an engine cowling and saw the shallow dent where it had struck the earth. As they walked, they met Captain Krack and another crew member, both talking to a survivor who was an amateur pilot.

Edmund Senkler listened to the conversation and added his own impressions. "It felt like someone had pulled down the rear flaps," he told the commander.

"Impossible!" Captain Krack shook his head. "Everything was normal. I can't understand what happened."

"There didn't appear to be any power failure," Edmund said.

Captain Krack agreed. He lapsed into a troubled silence, and that was the end of the conversation. They walked on, each alone with his thoughts.

10 • Missing

Tom Scott stood watching the fire, his emotions in turmoil. Part of him felt elated that he had managed to save so many people, and that he, too, had survived. But another part of him felt dark and depressed. He had noticed the tail section of the 747 lying in pieces all over the bush and knew, deep down, that all those friends who had drawn positions in the back of the aircraft had been killed. They could not possibly have survived.

He was standing there, occupied with bitter, sombre thoughts when an American woman came over to him.

"Now my trip is ruined!" the woman complained. "This crash has ruined everything."

Tom stared at her, momentarily speechless. A feeling of outrage overwhelmed him. "Lady," he retorted angrily, "you should be glad you're alive."

The woman walked away, and Tom Scott shook his head, thinking, maybe it's shock. It must be shock.

No one would behave like that normally.

Still shaking his head, Tom Scott walked over to see if he could help the ambulancemen caring for the wounded. While he was there, he observed that there were not many seriously injured people among the survivors. Most of those being helped were bleeding from cuts to the head, face and limbs, and there were others with fractures, dislocations, sprains and bruising, who were limping, holding their chests and backs, their faces contorted with pain. He helped as many as he could, walking them through the debris to the ambulances. When they had all gone he stood on the embanked road, staring numbly at the firemen pouring foam onto the wreckage.

A man in a car called out, asking if he wanted a lift to the airport. Tom looked at him and got into the car. There was nothing more he could do. He buckled the seat belt tightly across his hips and the car rolled slowly down the earth road towards the Mombasa highway.

"Please drive very carefully," Tom Scott pleaded. "I've just been through a really nerve-wracking experience."

"Don't worry," the man told him.

But Tom, feeling terribly nervous, repeated his request three or four times during the short journey to Nairobi airport.

The Land Rover came back up the hill to fetch us. The driver told us there was nothing more he could do down at the wreck; the firemen and ambulance crews had taken over.

Lynn and I helped our two sons into the back of the vehicle and climbed in next to them. It felt crowded. There were ten people squeezed into it, including the driver. He put the Land Rover in gear and we were bounced about as he took us across the bush and eventually steered onto the embanked earth road. It was smoother after that, but we still drove slowly.

Still on the embanked road, the Land Rover stopped almost in line with *Hessen*'s nose. The crash site was spread out to our left and, looking down from the extra height of the vehicle, I could follow the path the doomed 747 had taken. Directly in front of us, on top of the embanked road, there were torn pieces of metal and a shallow groove where the jet had gone over. Immediately beyond the road and below us was a dark oily smudge, marking the site of the first explosion. Strewn about the scorched earth was the wreckage of the tail section, in which so many people had been sitting. They had died here, on this spot, a few minutes ago. The rest of us had gone hurtling on, spun round and come sliding back to stop where the remains of *Hessen* now stood.

Wrecked seats, shredded clothing, suitcases and newspapers were lying everywhere. Sitting on a mound was the nun, who had sat in front of us on the 747, and a stewardess in her bright yellow uniform. Survivors were milling about, some climbing the side of the road.

"I can see dead bodies over there," my son Brendon called out.

"No, you can't," Lynn told him, her eyes even as she spoke shockingly aware of the sheer horror of the scene. But her whole being rebelled instinctively against focusing on anything other than her children. It felt to her as if she was living through a nightmare and that, soon, she would wake up, and everything would be all right again.

"I *can* see bodies," Brendon insisted. "Over there."

"Yes," Lynn acknowledged.

When Lufthansa purser Heidi Tischer saw our children in the Land Rover, she ran over in tears. "Have you seen the Mickey Mouse?" she asked. "We can't find the Mickey Mouse."

"No," Lynn told her. "The children were sitting with us."

"They weren't with the Mickey Mouse?"

"No, I'm sorry. They were with us all the time."

Heidi Tischer turned away, weeping.

From below, an American voice shouted, "Unitours? Anyone from the Unitours party?"

Renate Kahn shouted back the names of the Americans in the Land Rover. "We're five up here.

Karl, Nancy and Renate Kahn, and Gladys Golman and Tillie Harmel. Who have you got?"

A voice down below called out five names and there was some talk I could not make out.

"What did they say?" someone in the Land Rover asked.

"Three are missing," Renate told us. "The Solibakkes and Maya, our guide."

We fell silent. There was nothing we could say, nothing at all.

Our driver climbed back into the vehicle and slammed the door. "Everybody all right?"

"Yes," I said quietly, answering for us all.

The Land Rover's engine rumbled back to life and the wheels crunched over the wreckage on the road. We headed down the embanked road towards the Mombasa road and the airport.

The first of the ambulances sped back along the two-lane road to Nairobi, swerving out wildly to overtake slower moving traffic. Most of the cars were travelling the other way, driven by people attracted to the crash site by the dark column of smoke that could be seen from the city. The long line of cars coming head-on created a new hazard for the shocked survivors.

Dr Gerd Kampf-Emden held on as the ambulance he was travelling in swerved and braked. There was one other injured person in the speeding vehicle with him, but the two of them did not talk much. They were too nervous, waiting for the journey to be over.

Dr Kampf-Emden stared at his bleeding right foot, surprised that he had not felt any pain at the crash site. He was not even aware that he had been injured until his friend Hans Neeb pointed to the Lufthansa slippers he was wearing.

Kampf-Emden had worn the slippers so he could relax during the flight. When Hans Neeb pointed, Kampf-Emden looked down. He saw one slipper was covered in blood. His own shoes, he thought wryly, were probably ashes by now.

The ambulance carrying Margaret Hooker and Carol Mall was speeding along the same road, some distance behind Dr Kampf-Emden.

A little more than an hour earlier, the two women had travelled this road together, on their way to the airport to catch their flight. On that journey they had passed the time chatting about Carol's holiday in South Africa. But on this unexpected and unimaginable return journey Margaret Hooker sat in silence, staring at the limp body of the little girl in the jumper and wondering, "Is that child alive?" The child was deathly white and lay so still that Margaret found it hard to believe she was.

Carol Mall, lying on the other side of the ambulance, stirred. For a moment, the darkness in which she was trapped lifted, and she saw the roof of the ambulance and heard the siren screaming. Then she blinked her eyes and sank slowly back into darkness. It would be seven days before she woke again, and when she did, it would be to a completely different life.

Back at the crash site, Herbert Frosch and a group of helpers pulled a piece of board from the debris and carefully moved Bob Laburn onto it. An ambulance stopped close by and the small group of men lifted him up, carried him over and placed him in the back.

"You should lie flat out," someone suggested.

But Bob Laburn found that too painful. His half-reclining position may have looked peculiar, but it did reduce the throbbing pain.

The doors slammed and he was alone in the ambulance. He heard the ambulancemen getting into the front. There was a rumbling as the engine started, and the hell ride began. Each bump and rise and fall sent a jarring shock up his spine to the base of his skull. He closed his eyes and tried to minimise the movement, and the ride went on and on, the agony exploding with each lurch of the springs.

He heard the men talking. "This man has an injured back," he heard a voice say. "We must take him to the nearest hospital, not Nairobi."

The voices droned on ahead of him, but Bob Laburn concentrated on the swaying, leaning on his arm to lessen the impact. It didn't seem to help at all. How much longer? If only we were on a decent road, perhaps it would not be so bad.

He could not see where he was being taken, and he had no idea of distance or time. At times, it felt as if he had been travelling for hours over the bumpy road, but listening to the conversation of the ambulancemen, he thought it could have been only a few minutes. Probably we've not gone very far at all, he told himself, but this is almost certainly the worst journey of my life.

Suddenly, the ride became smoother and the ambulance stopped. He heard the men walking to the back, the doors opened and sunlight streamed in. He had arrived at the Mater Misericordiae Catholic mission hospital, a few miles from the crash site.

The men picked him up and carried him in, and the Irish and Kenyan sisters came hurrying up to examine him. Within a few minutes, Bob Laburn was settled on a bed, pleased that the ride was over, but anxious about his family in Johannesburg. He wanted to let them know he was alive.

He told Sister Leonard, who was making him comfortable, "Don't worry about me, but could you please telephone my wife or the Rand Water Board in Johannesburg and tell them I'm reasonably all right?"

The sister went off to see what she could do. Later she came back. She had been unable to get through.

The telephone lines to South Africa were jammed with callers.

That wasn't very surprising, Bob Laburn thought. Communications between the two countries weren't very good on normal days, never mind on days like this.

"Would it be possible for you to send a telegram to my office and tell them Bob Laburn is well?" he asked.

"Yes," the sister said. "I can do that."

He gave her the address and a rough wording, and off she went. After an hour she returned. The telegram had been sent, and his family and friends should hear the good news within an hour or so.

"Right," Bob Laburn said, "now you can deal with me."

The hospital's orthopaedic surgeon and a radiologist examined him carefully. He had three crushed dorsal vertebrae, some cervical spine difficulty, a crushed chest and some pneumonia in one lung. But he felt reasonably content now that news was on its way to his family. They would soon hear and stop worrying.

He had no way of knowing that his telegram would not arrive until a whole day later, and that neither hospital nor ambulance staff had reported his arrival at the mission hospital. For a long time his family and Lufthansa officials feared he was dead.

A bus drew up at the crash site and the survivors

straggled over and began climbing aboard. Edmund and Elinor Senkler sat down beside the nun, who had a red lump on her face and seemed troubled.

"Where are the sisters?" Mother Dietlinde Geis asked, referring to the four nuns from the Solanus Convent she had met at Frankfurt Airport.

Elinor Senkler reached out for Mother Dietlinde's hand and comforted her. The other sisters had been sitting in the rear compartment, and Elinor now knew that that part of the aircraft had been completely destroyed.

Across the aisle sat Captain Krack. He was holding his head in his hands, going over and over the details of the take-off with one of the passengers.

The seats filled up and the bus began moving off. As it drew level with the smoking wreck Captain Krack got up, stopped the bus and jumped off.

"I can't understand it," he muttered to himself again and again.

The survivors watched him walking back towards the wreckage with his head down on his chest. The bus moved off slowly.

11 • *Shock*

The car carrying Jock Leslie-Melville, Dancy Bruce and Esther Burton arrived at Nairobi Airport. The three of them got out and stood a few moments in silence, pale and shaken after watching the Lufthansa jumbo crashing in flames.

They looked for a porter to help them, but there was not a single one in sight. The porters, along with other airport employees were, at that moment, running across the bush to the scene of the burning 747.

Jock and the two young women picked up the luggage themselves and carried it into the terminal building. They dumped their bags in a heap in front of the check-in desk. But there was no one behind the desk. Then they noticed that there was no one behind any of the check-in desks.

Dancy looked around. Over at the coffee bar, the assistants had disappeared and the people in the lounge had climbed behind the bar to make their own coffee. No uniformed staff could be seen anywhere. What Dancy did see was people with expressions of horror on their faces walking up and down across the smooth stone floor. Some of these people were crying, holding the hands of friends, and covering their eyes.

Dancy, Esther and Jock were standing there, shocked, observing the chaotic scene, when a friend of Dancy's named Bruce Hobson walked up, holding a newspaper. He seemed upset.

"Bruce," Dancy said, holding onto him, "have you heard about the crash?"

"Yes," he said, looking at her. "I was on the observation deck . . . " His voice faltered and he stood in silence, shaking his head.

Bruce Hobson worked for a Nairobi safari company and, about an hour earlier, had escorted four German clients to the airport to catch the Lufthansa flight to Johannesburg. The clients were happy and relaxed, chatting and joking in the bus about their African holiday. No one seemed at all concerned about flying.

Bruce marshalled them through the check-in, helped organise their seats and luggage and directed them through immigration and customs. At the barrier there were handshakes, smiles and last-minute greetings, and the four Germans went walking off to board their flight. That was the last Bruce saw of them.

Bruce knew that in half an hour or so his friend Dancy Bruce would be catching her flight to London, so he decided to wait. He bought a newspaper and went up to the first floor observation balcony and sat reading in the early morning sunshine. Suddenly, he heard screams and shouts, and people on the balcony cried out and gasped. Bruce looked up and saw people crowding over to the right, pushing against each other to see something in the distance.

He jumped up from his seat. Beyond the heads of the crowd he saw a fire and thick, dark smoke billowing upwards. The 747's crashed, he thought, and then he realised . . . my clients, they're in that! He turned away in shock and hurried downstairs to find out what had happened and what he should do.

At the bottom of the stairs he found himself part of an astonishing scene. Ticket collectors, customs officers and every single airport and airline official, it seemed, was running through the baggage hall in the direction of the runway. Behind them came passengers and spectators, streaming through, dropping suitcases, bags and belongings all over the reception area as they ran. Above the shouts and cries of the frantic crowd Bruce heard the high-pitched, agitated voice of a woman announcing over the public address system that the Lufthansa jumbo jet had crashed.

As Bruce Hobson finished talking, Jock Leslie-

Melville had a sudden panicky thought: I should telephone Betty. She might hear something on the radio and think it was Dancy's plane.

He went off and found a telephone. "It was awful," he told his wife when he got through. "Terrible. I've never seen anything like it. All those people."

At first, Betty Leslie-Melville did not understand him. "What was it?" she asked. Her immediate thought was, it's a bus crash. Those awful roads.

"A jumbo," Jock said. "A 747's crashed at the airport."

"Oh, my God!"

Jock described what he had seen, the aircraft floating down, sinking, and the huge fireball appearing above the bush. "There just couldn't have been any survivors."

There was silence on the phone. Then Betty spoke. "What is Dancy going to do?"

"She says she'll go on to London. She feels it's unlikely there'll be two crashes on the same day, and I agree with her. They've closed the airport for the moment, but the runway isn't affected. They're sure to open it again soon." Jock paused, hearing the airport noises around him, and then he thought of something that hit him like a physical blow. He began to shake and a horrible cold shiver climbed up his back.

"Betty," he said hoarsely, "I've just realised. That could be the Moorhouses' plane."

Dancy Bruce's bags kept her place in the long line of people building up in front of the charter flight check-in desk. Some of the new arrivals, probably people who had not heard about the tragedy, were angry that their flight had been delayed. Arguments broke out and voices were raised.

"Look," Dancy heard someone saying, "you can't expect your plane to leave while they're still trying to find out what's happened to the one that's crashed."

Sickened by what she was hearing, Dancy strolled off to one side with Bruce Hobson and her friend, Esther Burton. Jock had left for his office in the centre of Nairobi to see what he could find out. Only minutes away from her flight, Dancy kept telling herself, it can't happen twice on the same day at the same airport. It just can't. The odds are totally against it. But she couldn't stop worrying and the sick feeling spread to her stomach. She knew this flight would be the worst she had ever been on. But she had to go, or she might never be able to climb into an aircraft again.

A group of doctors and nurses came hurrying into the airport and then, about forty minutes after the jumbo had gone down, Dancy saw the first survivors arriving.

A Land Rover drew up outside the airport entrance. It was splashed with mud and pieces of grass were sticking to the tyres. The doors swung open and a group of people got out and walked slowly into the airport. Leading them was a bizarre trio: two men and a woman, one of the men white-haired and deathly pale, and trembling so violently that the others had to hold him up. There was blood coming from his ears and dripping onto his shirt, and next to him walked a woman, tall and elderly, head up and smiling. There were cuts on their faces and they seemed to have fluff hanging in their hair and clinging to their shoulders and clothes.

More people came stumbling in from a second Land Rover. In this group was a stewardess, who was sobbing as she was being helped along, her bright yellow jacket clutched tightly to her, mud and blood staining her white blouse. The others with her walked unsteadily, their faces ashen, their eyes wide and staring. They, too, had fluff all over them, and some had torn clothing. As they walked, lumps of grassy mud fell from their shoes and stockinged feet, marking out a trail across the smooth airport floor.

A long-haired young woman came wandering by, both of her shoes missing, leading two young boys wearing jumpers. The three plodded on through the onlookers, passing close to Dancy, and it seemed they didn't know who to go to, or where to go, or what to do, or say. They appeared totally bewildered, horror showing in their silent faces, and Dancy felt, I should help them, or speak to them, or something. But she didn't know what to do, and stood numbed, watching them disappear into a different part of the airport building.

No more people came after the first two Land Rovers arrived, and Dancy thought with a sick, empty feeling, ten lucky people made it. Only ten.

Dancy was wrong. There were already seven survivors at the airport when the first Land Rovers drew up. Hermann Hennecke and his six German-speaking companions had arrived by car and were wandering about the building, looking for telephones. Their one thought was to let their families know they were alive. They were spotted by Taj Gulam, Lufthansa's passenger service manager for East Africa, who took them to a cafeteria off the departure concourse. Looking shaken himself, Taj urged them to sit down and relax at the small tables and order something hot to drink, at the airline's expense.

Hermann Hennecke and his companions sat down and a small team of first aid workers moved about, cleaning and dressing their scratches and wounds. Stewardesses waiting for the incoming British Airways flight joined the first-aiders, cleaning wounds and applying dressings. Taj Gulam walked about the tables with a clipboard and ballpoint pen and wrote down the survivors' names.

"If there is any close relative you would like us to

alive and shaken, yet still able to talk coherently to the amazed reporters.

There were touching scenes in the streets of Nairobi. Following an appeal broadcast by the *Voice of Kenya* radio station, hundreds of people gathered outside the city's blood donor centre to give blood for the injured survivors. They stood for several hours in the sun, people of all races, appalled by the tragedy that had occurred in the fields outside their city.

Simeon Njenga, the officer in charge of the centre, spoke movingly of their reaction. "The response has been wonderful," he told newsmen. "They are anxious to save the lives of their brothers and sisters."

People donated 528 pints of blood that day, but in the end, the hospitals' own blood banks supplied all that was needed.

telex, please give me the name and address," he said.

Hermann Hennecke wrote down his name and slipped out of the room. He walked down a passage, turned into an office and asked the man behind the desk if he could use the telephone.

"I have just survived the crash," Hermann told the man, "and I would like to contact my family, to tell them I'm okay."

"What crash?" the man asked in amazement. He had sat through all the announcements and turmoil and hadn't heard a thing.

When Hermann Hennecke told him, the man's eyes widened and he began to shake his head. He stared down at Hermann's feet. There was a ball of mud on each foot.

Hermann helped himself to the telephone directory, looked up his firm's Nairobi agent, and dialled the number. The man behind the desk went on staring dumbly at him.

Hermann heard the voice of Hartmeier, the local sales representative: "Who is that?"

"Hennecke, Olympia South Africa," Hermann answered. "My plane has just crashed."

The voice laughed in his ear. "You're a real joker!"

"No, this is deadly serious," Hermann insisted. "Will you please come to the airport. I must telephone my family in Johannesburg and Germany as soon as possible, and I don't think it will be possible from here. I've also lost my glasses."

The voice on the other end of the line was no longer laughing. "I'll be there in twenty minutes."

Hermann left the office. He walked through the airport building, not knowing where he was heading, or why. He saw a bar in a corner, went up and ordered himself a neat brandy. A man he had never seen before paid the bill. Hermann's money, along with his jacket and briefcase, were probably going up in smoke at that very moment.

Hermann felt the warmth of the brandy spreading through him and thought, it's only money. It could have been me.

Lynn and I wandered through the airport with our two sons and the five Americans from the Unitours party. Everything seemed remote and insubstantial. Even the sounds were dull and muted, as if someone had padded the place with cotton wool.

People were standing about, staring at us as we passed, but we were too shocked to feel self-conscious. We looked at the onlookers without really seeing them, and went on by, trapped in the turmoil of our minds. We were all moving jerkily and deliberately, taking giant strides, as if we were stepping over rolled-up carpets on the floor, and yet, at the same time, we felt almost as if we were floating.

The nurses helping the survivors in the cafeteria

knew why we were feeling so strange. Some of them came out to help us in. They put their arms around us, supported us, and sat us down at the tables. A British Airways stewardess in a pink uniform ran her hand over the boys' heads.

"Were they hurt?"

Lynn and I shook our heads. "No."

"Brendon was sleeping," Lynn told them.

"And you? Are any of you hurt?"

"My back's killing me," Lynn said, holding herself. "I think I've slipped a disk or something."

The stewardess looked alarmed and one of the nurses came over. While she was checking Lynn and the boys I examined myself. There was a cut on one of my fingers from the plastic ceiling and a gash on my leg, probably from hitting the seat in front of me when the jumbo struck the ground. I had my trouser leg pulled up to look and the stewardess saw the wound and said, "Oh, we must fix that up."

But it was nothing, the blood was already drying, and I told her, "Don't worry about it. It's all right."

But she insisted, went off and came back with a roll of plaster and a dressing, and I thought, well, let her put it on then, if it gives her something to do. She looks quite shaken.

"Thank you," I said, when she had finished.

She smiled. "And what about something to drink? Tea, coffee?"

We settled for tea, all of us, and sat without saying much. I watched the boys sipping and shook my head, trembling. What if one of them had died?

At one of the other tables sat the Kahns and, near them, Gladys Golman and her sister, Tillie Harmel, who was in great pain. Karl Kahn had ordered a coffee and brandy, but when it came, he was shaking so badly he couldn't get the cup to his mouth. It rattled against the saucer as he placed it back on the table. Renate, watching him, called over a doctor.

The doctor looked briefly at Karl and led him through to a small room close by to examine him. Karl's blood pressure had gone racing up and the doctor gave him an injection to calm him down. Karl relaxed and, after a while, felt much better. He got up and walked back to rejoin Renate in the cafeteria. His coffee had gone cold in the cup.

We heard a voice on the public address system saying that the airport was closed until further notice. Closed? It seemed odd that we had closed an entire airport.

Taj Gulam came up with his clipboard. I took his pen to write down our names and address, and the pen shook as I wrote on the paper. It did not look like my writing.

"How are you all?" he asked the boys. "Feeling

better?"

They stared at him blankly and didn't say anything.

"I want to go to the toilet," Garett whispered. I looked at the others, and discovered that we all needed to go.

"I'll take Garett, and you look after Brendon," I suggested to Lynn, and off we went, each holding a boy by the hand.

It took me a while to find the place, wandering about the building, the waiting passengers still watching us with those peculiar horrified expressions. We spotted the door and went in.

It was a multi-purpose room; in one corner there was a barber's chair and next to it stood a barber in a white outfit. He greeted us. There was another man with a mop and a bucket, and we were halfway across the room before I realised he had been washing the floor. It was still wet and we had walked over it in our muddy shoes.

"I'm so sorry," I apologised. "We've just come from the air crash, and I didn't think."

Both men looked startled.

"You have been in the jumbo jet?" the barber asked, his eyes wide.

"Yes, we managed to get out before it blew up."

The barber whistled, shaking his head. "You have been in that thing! Hei, you are lucky people!" He came over and shook our hands, and after him, the man with the bucket did the same.

"Please," the barber said, "take off your shoes. We will clean your shoes."

"No," I objected, "we can do it."

But he wouldn't stand for that. "We will do it," he insisted. "Come, give them to me."

So we took off our shoes and handed them over, and went through to the toilets. While we were in there we heard the two men talking, their voices echoing off the tiled walls. We washed our hands and faces and dried them, and when we came out I saw the men were wiping the last of the mud from the shoes with paper towels.

"It's very kind of you." I took my shoes and put them back on my feet, and helped Garett with his. "I'm sorry, I don't have any money. We lost everything."

The barber smiled and shook his head. "What happened?" he asked. "Why?"

"It came down," I said. "There wasn't enough power. I think the engines cut out, and we came down and hit the road. The jumbo broke in half and caught fire. We were just lucky. We were in the front half."

The barber made another whistling noise through his teeth and clasped my hand between both of his. "God is with you," he said. He did the same to Garett, and we both shook hands again with the cleaning man.

"Please, you must enjoy yourself now in Kenya,"

the barber said when we got to the door.

"Thanks very much," I said, feeling touched by it all.

Back in the cafeteria, I discovered that a busload of survivors had arrived, some wounded, some in torn clothing, and they were being treated by the medical team. At the table, Lynn reminded me, "Patricia and Ian will be waiting for us in Johannesburg. Can't we phone them, or something?"

"But they'll be at the airport."

"There must be someone we can phone. What about your mother? What about my mother?"

I looked out of the door and saw a small group of newsmen staring in, cameras slung from their shoulders, notebooks and pens in their hands. Before leaving South Africa for Europe I had worked as a sub-editor for the *Pretoria News*, and I remembered that the newspaper group to which it belonged had a correspondent based in Nairobi named Henry Reuter. If I could find him, perhaps I would be able to get a message to my former newspaper.

"I'll see what I can do."

I went over and asked the newsmen if they had seen Henry Reuter, or if he was around somewhere. They shook their heads, and began asking me questions: "What happened?" and "How did you get out?" and "Did you know it was going to crash?" and "How did it feel?" and so, and so on. I told them how it was, but I wasn't thinking clearly, and I was anxious to find Henry Reuter. I must have sounded really muddled. An airline official came out of the cafeteria, pulled me back into the room and told the newsmen to leave me alone.

"I'm trying to find a friend of mine," I said irritably, and sat down again at our table. I looked across at Lynn. "What's the matter with these people?"

She shook her head.

I went back to the doorway. The reporters were still waiting outside. They had been joined by television cameramen. A man in a grey suit came towards me, introduced himself, shook hands and said, "I believe you're looking for Henry Reuter?"

"Yes, is he here?"

"He's in Ethiopia. Something's brewing up there, and I've been asked to substitute for him."

"Oh, good," I said, pleased. "I'll give you a story if you do me a favour. I want you to telex the *Pretoria News*, and ask them to tell my family we've all survived."

"Certainly."

He wrote down the details, and I began telling our story . . . again.

Tom Scott spent about an hour wandering through the airport building, dazed. At first, he headed to the tea lounge. Then he changed his mind and decided he needed to visit the toilet. He headed back the other way, stopping to ask people, "Excuse me, do you know where the bathroom is?" They pointed out the way and he set off, but when he got there he didn't feel like going to the toilet any more. He turned and headed back to the cafeteria. At the cafeteria he decided he really had to go to the toilet. Off he went down the passageways, asking people for directions. He couldn't make up his mind what he wanted to do, so he continued wandering around the building.

When he finally returned to the cafeteria a British Airways stewardess handed him a cup of coffee. Holding onto something seemed to help, and he sat down with some of the other surviving crew members, and sipped slowly at the steaming cup, trying to understand why he was behaving so strangely. Later, he realised that it was all due to shock.

John and Jean Bing and Terry Partridge arrived at the airport building in a Land Rover driven by one of the Italian construction workers from the Sogene site. They walked into the cafeteria at the same time as Captain Krack and sat near him and the rest of the crew. Captain Krack was deeply distressed, and sat with his face in his hands, muttering and shaking his head. He kept looking up and asking, "Why?"

His surviving crew members stared blankly at him. Some shrugged, and one patted the captain's back, trying to calm him, but he would not be pacified.

Then everyone started getting up from the tables, some limping and being helped along, all of us stringing along in a line behind Taj Gulam and the other officials as they led us through the door.

"Where are we going?" someone asked.

"To the restaurant," a voice said from behind us. "Someone said they're going to give us a meal."

Lynn looked at me. "I don't feel like eating anything."

"Neither do I."

But we walked on in that peculiar procession of shocked, mud-stained, bloody and ragged people, and found ourselves being led through the back corridors of the airport building. We went up stairs, along corridors, and past closed doors, as if we were walking in a maze. It seemed a terribly complicated way of getting to the restaurant, and we couldn't understand why they took us that way. They might have been trying to keep us away from the newsmen and television cameras down on the departure concourse, but no one told us, and we kept on walking.

At one point, we came to a wet stretch of floor, and there was a man on his knees next to a bucket. He looked up, startled, and we halted. The officials spoke to each other, opened a door and led us a different way past the wet floor. Eventually, we arrived in a restaurant and were invited to sit down.

The officials began discussing something with the restaurant staff, and I guessed we would not have a meal there after all. Perhaps there were too many of us?

Taj Gulam was carrying his list of survivors from group to group. He had forgotten to list nationalities. I wrote "British" down next to our names, and he carried the list away.

When he returned, he announced that there would not be a meal at the airport. "We will take you to the Hilton and you can eat something there," he told us. "Please follow me."

The survivors filed out of the restaurant, heading onto a sunny balcony behind Taj Gulam and the officials, and walked down a flight of stairs to the ground floor. We were behind Mother Dietlinde, and came out through a side entrance into a car park and there stood a bus. We climbed aboard and found seats together.

When all the survivors were aboard, the bus started up, turned in the car park and headed onto the tarmac road, perhaps a little too quickly. I thought, "Too fast! He'll kill us all!"

The others were white-faced and tense, their hands gripping the seats. We were terrified of anything that moved.

The bus stopped at the junction with the Mombasa road. There was traffic speeding from left to right, in front of the bus, and I thought, "Oh no, I can't take much more of this." I tried not to look.

The bus began to swing out, turning right onto the road that led to the city centre, and a woman's anguished voice cried out from the back, "Please drive slowly! Please!"

12 • *One seat apart*

Doctors and staff at Nairobi Hospital had a routine start to their day that Wednesday morning. Then, at three minutes past eight, the day changed. The head nurse picked up the telephone and received a chilling message: "A jumbo jet has crashed. Prepare for a major disaster."

The head nurse left what she was doing and hurried through to the hospital's casualty department. An orthopaedic surgeon had just arrived, took the hospital's emergency "crash box" and, accompanied by a casualty nurse, raced off to the crash site. They were followed by the hospital's almoner, who was also a trained nurse, and a casualty officer.

The hospital team reached the site at eight thirty-five, about forty minutes after *Hessen* had struck the embanked road. By that time the firemen had the fire under control, but the wreckage was still burning, sending clouds of smoke into the air. The hospital team members surveyed the devastation and assessed what they could do to help. Most of the seriously injured survivors were being rushed to Nairobi by ambulance, but a few shocked survivors were wandering about near the embanked road, and the hospital team went forward to see if they needed medical attention.

At the hospital in Nairobi the off-duty casualty nurse had been called in and the School of Nursing was quickly converted into a receiving area for lightly injured survivors. The students were brought in from their lectures, and the hospital's consultants and general practitioners in the city were telephoned and asked to come and help as soon as possible.

Nairobi had not experienced a major air disaster before, and no one knew quite what to expect. Staff were worried that the small casualty department with its six couches would be overwhelmed by the numbers of injured. They had no idea how many there would be, but they were aware of the size of jumbo jets and thought apprehensively of the hundreds of passengers such an aircraft might be carrying.

Dr Gerd Kampf-Emden, the injured businessman who had been travelling in the first class cabin, was one of the first survivors to arrive. The ambulance he was being carried in came quickly up the road, and stopped outside the casualty department. He was helped in, still wearing his blood-soaked Lufthansa slippers.

He was impressed by the organisation of the hospital. The casualty team took him directly to a couch, eased off his slippers and socks, cleaned him up and gave him a pain-killing injection before stitching the two-inch gash in his foot. They dressed the wound and checked him for any other injuries and discharged him.

Outside, a driver gave him a lift to the West German Embassy. As the car began to move off he saw other ambulances arriving and numbers of people being helped into the building. Some were being carried on stretchers.

Among this group was Hans Offerbroich, who had severe multiple fractures. He was having difficulty breathing and arrived in a critical condition. Hospital staff rushed him through to intensive care. Some of those who arrived with him were suffering from serious neck and spinal injuries, as well as cuts and bruises. For a while the X-ray department was crowded as radiographers and nursing staff struggled to assess all the injuries, and more survivors were arriving as they worked.

Malcolm Solts was dropped off outside the hospital by Land Rover, and limped in with his legs bleeding and a number of painful bruises. He stayed at the hospital for about four hours while staff examined his throbbing right knee and ran a series of checks. He was told he had a torn ligament.

Malcolm Solts's treatment was interrupted while more seriously injured were rushed through, and he waited in the reception area. Due to the number of people crowding into it, this part of the hospital appeared chaotic. There were injured people everywhere, and he saw members of the cabin crew sobbing uncontrollably. Someone was screaming and demanding immediate attention, but most of the people seemed to be sitting or standing about, looking dazed and shaken, as if they couldn't believe this was really happening. There was no way of contacting family or anyone else; all the telephone lines were engaged. And people had no idea where they should go after they had been treated.

Later, airline officials arrived and organised transport to the Hilton Hotel for those who had been discharged, gave them money for clothes and essentials, and helped to arrange telephone calls. But for a long time at the hospital some survivors felt bewildered and abandoned.

The ambulance carrying Carol Mall and Margaret Hooker came through the city at speed, siren shrieking. The early morning traffic pulled over to let it through as it headed for the Kenyatta National Hospital. This was the only ambulance to arrive there. All the others went directly to Nairobi Hospital.

Carol Mall was unconscious and critically injured

with a broken neck. The doctors examining her found she was paralysed in all four limbs and had what looked like friction burns on her back, probably as a result of being pulled from the burning aircraft. In addition, she had a broken ankle, a broken thumb and cuts to her face. Hospital staff hovered about her all day as her body fought against massive shock and severe injuries.

The next day she was transferred to the intensive care unit at Nairobi Hospital and treated there for weeks before being flown out on a stretcher, heavily sedated, to the United States.

Several times in the weeks and months that followed Carol's life hung in the balance, due to complications arising from her injuries. She developed a stress ulcer, haemorrhaging so severely that she needed sixteen pints of blood in one day, and doctors were forced to perform emergency surgery.

Following her return to Washington DC, she developed pneumonia, suffered a near cardiac arrest and spent six weeks in an intensive care unit. After a year and a half in hospitals and nursing homes her condition stabilised, but it was clear that the combination of her injuries and disability made it unlikely she would ever return to what passes for a normal life.

Also at the Kenyatta National Hospital that Wednesday morning, Carol's rescuer Margaret Hooker had her foot and arm wounds neatly stitched by a doctor. Strangely, she had bled very little and guessed this was because she had been covered in jet fuel. An injection numbed the pain, but she felt dazed, almost anaesthetised, by the horror of what she had been through. Her mind wandered as the doctor treated her. Confused, troubled and saddened, she struggled to make sense of what had happened. How could one? She and Carol had sat side by side, only one seat apart, but what a tragic difference that had made. She had staggered away from the wreckage, badly wounded, but it seemed that poor Carol might be paralysed and never walk again . . . all because of the seats they had been allocated by a helpful man in the airport terminal.

After Margaret's wounds had been dressed and bandaged, she was driven along tree-lined streets to Nairobi Hospital to spend the night. She was hardly aware of the trees, or the route they were taking. Her mind was occupied by the thought that, if the aircraft had not crashed, she would by now have been driving instead down the streets of Johannesburg.

The orthopaedic surgeon who had returned from the crash site quickly rejoined the casualty team at the hospital. He had a busy morning. Nearly all the seriously wounded had fractures and needed orthopaedic treatment. The surgeon noted a high incidence of spinal injuries. Five passengers and two crew members had fractures or strains of the lower back, a result of sitting strapped in, head dropped down between the knees in the crash position, while the jet went hurtling into the earth faster than an express train. Six others were brought in with whiplash injuries to the neck, and three people had both neck and back strain.

By mid-afternoon fifty-five survivors had been treated, including one passenger who had no injuries but was treated for shock, and eight crew members. Twenty-three had been admitted. Among those needing attention was the flight engineer, Rudi Hahn, who had his dislocated shoulder reduced. Co-pilot Schacke was treated for cuts to the head. Five of the crew were admitted.

One thing that surprised hospital staff was that not one of the people they treated had been burned.

Newsmen wandered through the wards looking for survivors who would talk to them. In St George's Ward they found Captain Heinz Peper, who had been sitting in the rear of *Hessen*. He was the only survivor from the tail compartment. Of all the escapes that day, his was perhaps the most miraculous.

He told reporters, "I could see from the very start of the take-off run that something was wrong. By the time we were halfway down the runway it was clear to me that we were travelling too slowly."

He had sat staring out, watching the runway blurring past, and it had seemed to him as if the 747 had lifted only at the very end of the runway. Then, after taking off, the jumbo jet began to shudder.

"I knew this was it," the young captain said quietly. "I lowered my head between my legs in the emergency position and waited for the crash. Seconds later, we were shaken by the first impact.

"I can't remember exactly what happened then, except that the seats and passengers in front of me disappeared into a big crack at my feet. My section of the plane was thrown sideways and I lost consciousness."

He paused, thinking. "I don't know how long I was blacked out, but when I woke up, I saw a huge hole in the fuselage next to where I was sitting. I undid my seat belt and fell head-first out of the crack."

He landed in a field of fire, the grass around him burning fiercely. He struggled to his feet and blacked out again. When he recovered consciousness he scrambled to his feet and ran for his life.

"I had not gone twenty-five metres before a huge explosion knocked me flat," Captain Peper remembered.

The blast wrecked the compartment he had been sitting in, hurling flaming wreckage across the bush. The explosion and fire killed all those he had been sitting with a few moments before. But there he was,

13 • *Waiting for news*

In Britain some people heard the news before breakfast. At seven that Wednesday morning, BBC news readers reported that there appeared to be no survivors of the world's first jumbo jet disaster, which had occurred at Nairobi, in Kenya.

Among the millions who heard the news broadcast was the secretary of Sheffield sales engineer Terry Partridge. She was numbed by a sudden shocking realisation: they were talking about the flight her boss was on. He had been booked for an economy return flight from Manchester via Frankfurt to Johannesburg for a two-week sales trip to South Africa to seek orders for his firm's heat-resistant materials.

Badly shaken by the news, she telephoned Terry Partridge's boss and the two of them discussed what they should do. What *did* one do at a time like that? It was too early to telephone Terry's wife. It was unlikely she would be awake. They decided to wait, and send someone round to the house at nine o' clock, by which time there would probably be more news. They hung up, listening apprehensively for the next news update on the crash. When it came, they heard there were now estimated to be no more than fifty survivors.

Jill Partridge had returned from taking her six-year-old daughter Sarah to school and was starting the household chores at her home in Worrall, close to Sheffield, when she heard some people arrive at the door. It was Terry's business colleague, Colin Atson, and his wife, Vera.

"Come in," she told them cheerfully. She thought, Vera's probably not feeling too well and has come to spend the day with me.

Once inside, the Atsons asked Jill to sit down and said they had something to tell her. She looked at them and sat down, suddenly anxious.

"The plane that Terry was on has crashed."

She heard what they were saying, but could not believe it.

"It was only half full, and about half the people have survived. So there's a good chance that he's all right."

Jill sat numbed, distressed by the thought of Terry in a crashing aircraft. Then she told herself, no, I'm sure he's all right. He *must* be all right. It was a desperate, illogical thought, but she felt quite sure that he was alive.

There was little anyone could do but wait for more news. Jill sat there, comforted by the Atsons and doing her best to reassure her three-year-old daughter Helen, who seemed to know that her mother was upset.

Jill telephoned her sister and they discussed telling their parents what had happened. They decided it would be better to wait until they heard something definite. Jill put the phone down, wanting to keep the line clear for any news.

The minutes dragged by. Ten, twenty, thirty, forty minutes. All that time her mind was in a whirl and she repeated to herself, I'm sure, so sure, that he's all right.

At that moment, thousands of miles away in Nairobi, Terry Partridge was stepping off a bus that had brought survivors to the Hilton Hotel from the airport. He walked into the lobby and went directly to the reception desk.

"I want to send a telex message to England," he said. "I've just been in the jumbo crash."

It was arranged in minutes.

The telephone rang in Worrall. Colin Atson stepped over and picked it up. It was from his office. A few minutes ago, a telex message had been received from Nairobi: Terry Partridge was alive and unhurt and checking in at the Nairobi Hilton.

Jill Partridge burst into tears, and young Helen cried, too. Jill held her daughter to her, sobbing with relief after the most wonderful telephone call of her life.

In Johannesburg, news of the disaster spread, and shocked families began an agonising wait for information about their loved ones. Gisela Hutton was at home, dressed and ready to leave for the airport. She was waiting for her husband to arrive so they could travel together to meet her eighty-eight-year-old father, Erich Hesse, who was flying in for a few weeks' holiday.

When her husband arrived, he appeared shaken and upset. He had telephoned the airport to check the arrival time of the Lufthansa flight and had been told there would be a delay "of uncertain duration". Worried, he telephoned a friend, the editor of the Johannesburg *Star*, and learned that the aircraft had crashed at Nairobi.

Others heard while they were waiting at the airport. Anna Eybers screamed and collapsed on the concourse. Her daughter Petro and son-in-law Manfred Fischer were aboard the Lufthansa flight, returning home to their children, Werner, aged seven, and Helane, five, at the end of a working holiday in Germany.

Later, when she had recovered from her initial shock, she went home with her grandchildren. The children tried to cheer her up, telling her their mother and father would return eventually. Listening to them almost broke Anna's heart.

That afternoon she heard that both Petro and Manfred had survived, and told journalists, "November the twentieth is the most wonderful day I can remember."

Later, as more details became available, her daughter's name was removed from the list of survivors, but Manfred Fischer was said to be alive and at the Hilton Hotel. Despairing and confused, Anna waited, praying that it was all due to a bureaucratic muddle, and that when the official list of survivors was issued the names of both Petro and Manfred would be on it.

"Petro didn't want to go on vacation to Germany," she told a reporter. "At the last minute she asked me if I wanted to go in her place. She wasn't even interested in packing her suitcase and only finished when I helped her."

The hours passed, and still there was no news. Anna Eybers was forced to wait through the night. In the morning officials told her both Petro and Manfred were dead.

At the Holy Childhood Convent in Eshowe, Zululand, the days of waiting were almost over. Their mother superior was coming back from home leave in Germany.

The convent children were jumping up and down with excitement as Sisters Edith, Elkana and Martina climbed into the Volkswagen combi that would fetch

Mother Dietlinde from the airport in Durban. She would be arriving there after changing flights in Johannesburg.

The engine sparked into life, and the sisters waved as their van went carefully down the dusty road on its way to Durban.

On the way, the three sisters stopped to buy school exercise books for the next school year, and called later at the Mari Stelle Mission to pick up Sisters Liboria and Theodelind, who had decided to travel with them to greet Mother Dietlinde. The five women reached Durban airport half an hour after midday and heard a voice announcing over the public address system that the connecting flight from Johannesburg had been delayed by fifty minutes.

Back at the Eshowe convent that the sisters had left a few hours earlier, a telephone call came through from Germany. It was from Mother Ehrengarda, speaking from Wurzburg-Oberzell, where Mother Dietlinde had spent her home leave.

The jumbo jet carrying Mother Dietlinde had crashed at Nairobi, Mother Ehrengarda reported. The news had been flashed on German radio and television a short while ago. No one knew if anyone had survived.

The news spread quickly through the Eshowe convent and its school. Children burst into tears and the sisters called an immediate midday break.

Everyone went into the church to pray.

At Durban airport the delayed aircraft finally landed at one-fifty in the afternoon and the sisters stood waiting expectantly for their first sight of that familiar figure. Fifteen passengers got off, but Mother Dietlinde was not among them.

The sisters were on their way to the information desk to find out what had happened when they saw the mother superior from the Mari Stelle Mission and another sister approaching. Telephoned by the nuns of Eshowe, the mother superior had decided to drive to the airport herself with the dreadful news. Now, grim-faced, she told them, "Mother Dietlinde's aeroplane has crashed at Nairobi."

Officials at the information desk suggested to the shocked nuns that they should drive to the Lufthansa office in Durban for more news. They did so and, when they arrived, they were told it was now known that ninety-one people had survived the crash. Twenty-one were being treated in the Nairobi Hospital, and the others had been booked in at the Hilton Hotel. So far, there were only fifty names on the airline's list of identified survivors.

Was there a Geis among them?

The officials checked. Yes, there was a Geis, a Mr Geis.

The sisters looked at one another, wondering what

this meant. They discussed it, and decided to wait. There was still hope. It was possible there had been a mistake. Perhaps the person listed as Mr Geis would eventually turn out to be Mother Dietlinde.

After three hours of waiting, the telephone rang again at the Holy Childhood Convent in Zululand. It was Mother Ehrengarda, calling once more from Germany.

"Mother Dietlinde is among the survivors!" she said.

Sister Urbana clutched her skirts and went running off towards the school. The children and sisters in the school heard her excited shouts coming nearer. "The mother is alive! She is alive!"

At midnight in Johannesburg, Beryl Laburn was still waiting for news of her husband, Bob. An airline official working through the night telephoned to give final confirmation that Bob Laburn was not on the list of survivors. It should be presumed that he was dead.

The news came as a shattering blow to Beryl and her family. Until then they had held out hope that, in the confusion following the accident, Bob's name had been overlooked, and would eventually appear.

The family's telephone calls throughout the day to Lufthansa's Johannesburg office and to the Rand Water Board, where Bob worked, had told them nothing more. Bob Laburn was not among the survivors, nor was he among the dead who had been identified. It was possible that he was one of the charred corpses awaiting identification in the Nairobi City Mortuary, or that his body was still hidden in the burned-out wreckage.

In her anguish, Beryl Laburn clung to one last hope. Someone, she knew, had tried to telephone her that day at her office, but had failed to get through. This small unexplained event gave her something to cling to in those dark hours of the early morning.

As morning broke that Thursday, the flag on the Rand Water Board building overlooking the Library Gardens in Johannesburg was lowered to half-mast as a mark of respect. People noticed it as they hurried past on their way to work.

Soon after nine o' clock, a telegram arrived and was taken in to the Water Board's secretary. It stated that Bob Laburn had back injuries, but was reasonably well and in the Misericordiae Hospital in Nairobi. There was a telephone number.

The secretary did not know what to think. The telegram had been sent at about eleven o' clock the previous day. Should he accept this, or should he accept Lufthansa's much later news, that Bob Laburn was dead?

He decided to try the telephone number.

The call that came through from Johannesburg puzzled the sisters at the Misericordiae Hospital. But they did what the caller asked. They went through and asked their patient to tell them the names of his wife and children.

Lying in his hospital bed, Bob Laburn was indignant. What did the hospital want personal information like that for? And then he became apprehensive: perhaps something had happened at home. He gave them the information, wondering what it was all about.

At the other end of the line in Johannesburg, the Water Board secretary received the information and shouted out, "Bob's alive! It's all been a mistake!"

Bob Laburn's colleagues let out a cheer, and a short while later the flag on the building was run up to the top of the mast.

It was already mid-morning before Beryl Laburn heard the news, and she wept with relief and joy.

Bob Laburn's name had been on the survivors' list all along, the family heard, but it had been written down incorrectly. There was no such person as "Mr L A V Bern", but on that morning no one was complaining. Bob Laburn had come back from the dead.

14 • *Survivors*

At the Hilton Hotel, survivors crowded round the telephones in the lobby as they struggled to put through international calls to relatives and friends.

For the four of us, it felt strange to be in Nairobi after we had prepared ourselves mentally for an arrival in Johannesburg. We wandered about, feeling lost, and I kept thinking there was something I should be doing, but I could not guess what it was.

Lynn was holding her back and wanted to keep walking, because it hurt her to stand still, and I kept urging her to see a doctor. Through all of this, our two sons clung to us, and people kept coming over to touch them and fondle their hair. The boys seemed unusually quiet and bright-eyed.

We were a strange-looking group of people in our torn and blood-stained clothes, some of us bandaged, some missing shoes. The porters stared at us. There was nothing for them to do. None of us had any luggage.

A telephone call brought our Nairobi friends, Jock and Betty Leslie-Melville, to the Hilton, and it was a tearful meeting. They had spent hours trying to find out what had happened to us, and now here we were, shaken, but virtually untouched.

From our hotel room overlooking the city, we could see the sun shining brightly on the buildings, and we tried to relax. Betty went off to buy us new toothbrushes and a facecloth, and that gave us another shock: we didn't even own a toothbrush! All we had were the clothes we were wearing.

Elsewhere in the hotel, Malcom Solts returned from receiving treatment at the hospital and managed to get a call through to his wife Andrea in Boston. In faraway Massachusetts, the telephone rang at six-fifteen in the morning and woke her up. Due to the time difference, she hadn't even heard about the crash.

Lufthansa steward Tom Scott went out shopping and bought himself a new toothbrush, a razor and shaving cream, and then, because there was nothing else to do, he went swimming in the Hilton pool. Afterwards, he lay basking in the sun and thought how odd it all was, that life could simply go on as usual after what had happened a few hours ago. He had come close to dying. Yet here he was, lying beside a pool, behaving as if none of it had taken place, while his mind filled with feelings he couldn't express.

Tom was in deep shock, but did not realise it. Two mornings later he suffered an episode of uncontrollable trembling and couldn't keep down any food. By the afternoon he felt he was losing consciousness. A strange tingling passed through his body and he lost control of his actions. He was terrified, and wondered what was happening to him. Eventually, the shaking subsided and he felt calmer. He worried that it might happen again, but it never did.

It was lunch time. Lynn had gone off to the hospital to have her back checked and I went down to the ground floor restaurant with my two sons.

"You can have anything you like," I told them, "because today's such a special day."

"Anything?" Garett asked.

"Whatever you like. You choose."

"Even ice cream?"

"Even ice cream."

They ordered two huge plates from the waiter and I watched them spooning it up, making it last, and thought how lucky we were to be able to sit there and eat.

I was struggling over something more substantial, finding it difficult to eat, and looked up as someone came through the door. I stared hard, not really believing my eyes. It was the elderly man who had been sitting in the seats behind us on the 747, the man I had thought was dead. He couldn't possibly have got out in time, but here he was, walking into the restaurant, alive, with a bloody dressing on his forehead.

I jumped up and shook his hand. "Am I pleased to see you!"

He showed me his attache case and took out his passport. I read his name: Erich Hesse.

"We thought you were dead."

He smiled and shook his head. He spoke only German, but he understood. He had survived.

Evening fell over Nairobi, the orange of the sunset fading swiftly from the horizon. Hermann Hennecke was speaking on the telephone to his wife and children in Johannesburg.

"I'm fine," he was telling them. "And I'll be home as soon as I can get a plane out of here."

"Do we have to go to school in the morning?" asked seven-year-old Ralf, and he heard his father chuckling at the other end of the line.

In a restaurant in a different part of the Hilton, the ten surviving American members of the Unitours safari group were meeting to decide whether to continue their trip, or return home.

They sat in a room hung with African spears and

shields and zebra skins, wearing the same clothes they had crashed in, and talked quietly. They all wanted to go on with the tour. There didn't seem to be any sense in heading home; they were already in Africa. But they missed the smiling face of their guide, Maya Galitzine, and the quiet companionship of the Solibakkes.

An orchestra gathered to play for the evening's dancing and the smell of steaks frying over charcoal wafted through. Cooks in white hats bent over the sizzling food as music began to play.

Elinor Senkler suddenly remembered the special dinner she and Edmund had planned to have in Johannesburg on this night. Twenty-six years ago today . . .

"Eddie," she reminded him, "it's our anniversary."

There were congratulations from the group.

"We must celebrate!" someone called out.

Soon champagne corks were popping and the Senklers were being toasted. Smiling waiters carried in trays of lobsters caught in the Indian Ocean, and the evening took on a festive air. There were interruptions: newsmen visited the table for interviews, and from time to time members of the group were called away to answer telephone calls from the United States.

On it went into the night. Listening to the music and the voices around her, Elinor Senkler thought, this is more than an anniversary. What we're really celebrating is today's miracle, the miracle that we're alive.

Several floors above the restaurant, I lay with Lynn in the half-dark of our hotel room, trying to sleep. The telephone kept ringing. There was a call from a journalist in Melbourne, Australia, and several calls from newsmen in London. The Argus newspaper group in South Africa phoned, asking me to cable an exclusive survivor's account of the crash in the morning.

We lay there, exhausted, but unable to sleep. We could see Garett and Brendon through the connecting doorway to the next room, sleeping on their beds, two small dark heads against the white of the pillows.

There was a sudden cry. Garett jumped up from the bed, shouting, "Get out! Get out!" He ran wildly round the room, and climbed over the furniture.

Shaken, Lynn and I ran through. We caught him at the door, tugging desperately at the handle, sobbing, "We've got to get out! Get out!"

Lynn held him against her. "It's all right, darling. You're only dreaming."

As he tried to fight free, I saw his face. He was terrified, his eyes glazed, and it was as if we were not there. We led him back to bed, stroking his forehead, talking gently, and after a long time it seemed that he had drifted off to sleep.

We went back to our bed and lay down, still

watching him through the doorway.

"Did you see his eyes?" Lynn whispered. "He couldn't see us. Do you think he's all right?"

"I don't know."

A while later it happened again: the frantic rush to the door, the shouts, the tears. We quietened him again, but we couldn't sleep after that. We were waiting for the next time.

I lay on my bed and wondered what on earth the crash had done to him. What does a thing like that do to six- and seven-year-olds?

The lights still glowed in the Nairobi City Mortuary as officials worked on, trying to identify the fifty-nine shrouded bodies spaced out on the floor. Many had been disfigured by fire and the only clues about their identity came from charred passports, watches and jewellery, which had been labelled, numbered and stored in transparent plastic bags.

Most of the victims died on impact, the pathologists decided, flung out or fatally injured as they sat strapped to their seats. In most cases, the pathologists believed, death had come from other injuries before burning. Nine people had died from smoke asphyxiation, and seven had sustained severe injuries which would have prevented them from escaping.

Another eleven died from burning, and nine of these had been trapped in the aircraft by injuries and unable to move. Their bodies were found in the forward half of the aircraft, among the burned-out remains of the economy class "quiet" section and the first class compartment.

The next day a non-scheduled Lufthansa Boeing 707 taxied out for take-off, carrying a group of survivors, who were returning to Germany. Among them was Dr Gerd Kampf-Emden, his foot heavily bandaged.

There was total silence as the aircraft turned in the stopway. The passengers looked pale and nervous. It must have taken a lot of courage to fly again twenty-four hours after the crash, Dr Kampf-Emden thought, mentally detaching himself for a moment from the rest of the group.

And then the take-off roll began.

No one spoke. Hands tightened across stomachs, clasped armrests. The aircraft hurtled faster and faster down the runway. Some people instinctively bowed their heads. Some shed tears.

The nose lifted, the 707 hung there for seconds, and rose steadily up into the morning air. Passengers sat with eyes closed, remembering what had happened the day before. This time they felt the surge of power pressing them back against their seats.

Minutes later, the aircraft levelled off, thousands of feet up, the nose aimed for Frankfurt and home.

Stewardesses came down the aisles, carrying trays of champagne, and soon the survivors were swapping tales with each other and the cabin crew. Laughing and relaxed, they flew on.

Dr Kampf-Emden looked down at his glass filled with light, sparkling bubbles. They had all faced death together. There was a bond between them that would remain long after the champagne had gone and the flight was over. It was wonderful to be alive and going home, but underlying it all he felt a deep and bitter sadness. He could not stop thinking about those whose lives had ended on the muddy fields of Nairobi.

15 • *Breakdown*

When I woke up the next morning I felt strange. I lay in bed, moving my head slowly on the pillow, staring at the walls, then the windows, then the furniture in the hotel room. My mind kept slipping back to the events of the crash. Even as I came out of sleep, all I could think about was that only a morning ago, at about the same time, our jumbo jet was starting its roll down the runway. Everybody on it was still alive. Seconds later it was crashing and breaking apart in flames, and people were dying. We had escaped, and it was difficult to understand why. It didn't make sense that we should still be here, alive, when so many others were dead. All those children . . .

A dark chill passed through me. Our two sons could have been among them. If they had accepted the invitation of the Mickey Mouse stewardess, they would have been sitting in the tail section with the other children, waiting for the story she had promised them. First the take-off, then the story. But our sons weren't interested. They had wanted to stay with us. So they said no . . . and survived.

But what if they *had* been interested? They would have been sitting there, without us, through the terror of the shaking aircraft. What would they have seen?

Lynn was awake next to me, and I asked, "How do you feel?"

She shook her head. "I don't know." Her voice was barely a whisper.

The boys woke up and we all dressed in the only clothes we had and went downstairs to the restaurant for breakfast. We ate quietly, not saying much. From our table we could see some survivors gathering in the lobby for transport to the airport. I watched them in silence, wondering how they could possibly climb into an aircraft and take off so soon after what had happened. Just thinking about it made me feel ill, so I looked away. And when I looked at the lobby again, they had all gone.

One of those who left that morning was Sheffield businessman Terry Partridge. The shocking events of the previous day had taken their toll, and it was his impression that he had not slept at all during his night at the Hilton. But when he got out of bed, he felt well enough and decided to fly on to Johannesburg and continue his business assignment.

His flight south that morning was an anxious one,

but as Terry Partridge walked through the arrivals hall at Johannesburg's international airport a few hours later he thought he had coped reasonably well. Some time afterwards, he began to feel shaky, and the feeling worsened steadily throughout the day. Eventually, he went to see a doctor, who prescribed a course of sedatives.

The next day he felt even worse and burst into tears while speaking to his wife Jill on the telephone. He decided to cut short his trip and fly back to Britain as soon as he could get on a flight.

Back home again, he was still deeply upset. Several mornings he woke up sobbing for no apparent reason and felt depressed. He went to to see his doctor and, while trying to explain what was wrong with him, broke down in the consulting room. It was one of the worst times he could remember.

His doctor prescribed a two-month course of strong sedatives and advised him not to travel for a while. The two months were hell. He recalled later, "My nerves were pretty shot and I couldn't really function or talk to anybody for any period of time without getting upset. But I took the tablets and at the end of two months I seemed to be back to almost normal."

At about the time Terry Partridge was flying south to Johannesburg, I was walking through the early morning streets of Nairobi to the office of Henry

Reuter, correspondent for the Argus newspaper group. I was going there to write a survivor's account of the crash.

As I walked, I felt strange, and knew something wasn't right. I wondered, am I going mad? I seemed to taking gigantic steps down the pavement, as if someone was placing objects in front of me, and I had to raise my knees high to get over them. Puzzled, I looked down at my legs, and it felt as if I had grown taller, and was seeing my limbs from a great height. There was a vagueness to everything, as if I was seeing life through tinted glasses. My neck seemed stiff, too, and I had to turn my whole body in order to look to my left or my right. How odd, I thought. What's happening to me?

I plodded on and eventually reached Henry Reuter's office. Back after reporting on something in Ethiopia, he shook my hand, made a cup of tea and sat me at a desk behind a typewriter. A long roll of carbon-backed three-ply paper was positioned in the machine.

"I'll tear it off as you go along," he said.

I looked at him. "Is there any special angle you want?"

He shook his head. "Why don't you just start at the beginning, and go on till the end. Tell us what happened and how it felt."

I sat with elbows on the desk, put my head in my hands and closed my eyes. I stayed like that for about a minute, thinking. From a distance, I heard Henry Reuter's voice asking, "Are you all right?" He sounded concerned.

I nodded, "Yes", opened my eyes and began typing:

"The horror of the Nairobi air crash was that most of us knew the moment the wheels lifted from the runway that the jumbo jetliner would come down. "

I wrote for about twenty minutes, only half aware of what I was doing. I was back in the shuddering aircraft with Lynn and the boys, and it was nightmarish. Every few paragraphs, I hammered the carriage return a few times, so Henry Reuter could tear off the story in sections, and rush each page through to a typist who was copying it for transmission.

By the time I had finished, I was exhausted. I left the office in a daze and walked slowly back to the Hilton. I reached the hotel room and saw the boys, and Lynn came over and held me and asked, "Was it very difficult?" I could only nod as tears filled my eyes.

In the morning, when I woke, my body was shivering. It must be a cold, I thought, or the beginning of flu. I didn't feel like eating, so Lynn went down to the restaurant with the boys to have breakfast, leaving me in bed. By the time they got back, I was shaking uncontrollably, my stomach was churning and my breathing was rapid and shallow. That strange vagueness had returned. My head ached and I felt fluttery and frightened. Was I seriously ill? Perhaps my head had smashed into the seat-back harder than I thought when the jet struck the ground?

Lynn said, "I think we should get a doctor to take a look at you."

She made a phone call, and about an hour later a doctor arrived. He had been sent by the airline. I was trembling so badly that my teeth were chattering as he examined me. My condition was not serious, he said, possibly a mild fever that would soon pass. He gave me some tablets and left. I managed to get two down my throat, and fell asleep.

When I woke up a few hours later, the terrible shaking had stopped and for a while I felt almost normal again.

The next day was Saturday and I felt well enough to go shopping for a pair of socks, using money Lufthansa had given us to buy clothes and essentials. I walked out of the shop, carrying the new socks in a paper bag. As I reached the street, there was a sudden roar. A dark aircraft shape came swooping down. My heart faltered. I barely had time to cry out, and staggered back against the shop window. The dark shape almost touched me as it passed. Then I realised, it's a shadow. The actual aircraft, a large low-flying four-engined turbo-prop machine, disappeared over the rooftops.

I walked back to the Hilton feeling shocked that I had been frightened by a shadow. And I knew then that it would take a lot longer before I recovered fully from what had happened aboard *Hessen*.

A day later, while we were being driven back into Nairobi in a car, after spending time outside the city with our friends, Jock and Betty Leslie-Melville, Lynn suddenly squeezed her eyes shut, ducked her head and broke down in tears. She had been struggling for days to hold herself together, and had been unable to cope one moment longer with the sensation of yellow-brown grass blurring past on both sides of the car. It reminded her too horribly of our 747's headlong rush down the runway.

Sitting in the back, I drew her close, trying to provide some comfort, but she could not stop weeping, even though she knew it was upsetting the boys.

When we arrived back at the Hilton we went up to our rooms and I closed the curtains so Lynn could sleep. While she did, I played with our sons in the next room, looking through the connecting door from time to time to check on her.

An hour or so later, she appeared in the doorway and said she was feeling much better.

Within a matter of days most of the survivors had flown out of Nairobi. But a few, like us, were still at the Hilton, feeling tearful, bewildered and confused, and suffering from an inability to make decisions. In a way, it seemed enough simply to have survived. We could all so easily have died.

Eventually, apart from critically injured Hans Offerbroich and Carol Mall, we were the only survivors left in the city, and airline officials wanted to know what our plans were.

The truth was, we did not know. We were in a strange situation. Having failed to change our excursion tickets so we could get off the flight in Nairobi, we had resigned ourselves to spending a week or two in Johannesburg. Then we crashed. And suddenly, in the most frightening and horrific circumstances, we found ourselves where we had originally wanted to be . . . in Nairobi.

But everything had changed. We didn't feel right. At first we felt numb. Then we felt shocked. The shock went on for a long time, and we weren't even aware of it. It made us feel bewildered and sad, so sad that we broke down in tears. Another thing we felt was guilt, that we were alive and others had died. We felt afraid, and vulnerable, anxious, angry and, surprisingly, lonely.

The mood swings alarmed me. So did my lack of judgement, and my inability to decide anything. Why had I changed? What was happening to me? And, feeling like I did, how could I possibly take on a new job, set up an office and communications network, and provide the services people were expecting from me?

I did not want to admit it, but I was in no condition to launch or manage anything. All I wanted was for someone I trusted to tell me what to do. And so I did nothing. I waited. For what? I had no idea.

We walked in the streets, and bought a few essentials. But even in the streets there was no escape. Near the Hilton Hotel, photographs of the crash were displayed in the windows of a newspaper office. They included an image of us walking with fellow survivors at the airport, and another, taken while we were being interviewed. These pictures had also appeared in the local newspaper. Because of our sons, we were easily recognised and strangers stopped us in the street to ask questions and stroke the boys' heads. They were the youngest survivors and became the centre of attention as people crowded around us. We were asked to tell the story again and again, and each time we were forced to relive the nightmare. It was exhausting, and I couldn't help wondering, would it ever end?

Then, one morning, an express letter arrived from our sister-in-law, Patricia Horsfield, in Johannesburg. "Please please come back soon," she pleaded. "It's so terrible not being able to see you."

She described what had happened to them, and we pictured it in our minds, Patricia and Lynn's brother Ian, and their young son Timothy walking across the arrivals hall at the airport, with everything at that moment seeming normal, and then staring at the indicator board, and their expressions changing to puzzled frowns when they discovered that the Lufthansa flight from Frankfurt had been delayed indefinitely. *Indefinitely?* What did that mean? And while they stood there a newspaper reporter approached and asked if they had relatives on board. The aircraft, he told them, had crashed at Nairobi.

We felt choked when we read her words. She described their frantic drive into Johannesburg, to the airline office. A nightmare journey. When they arrived, they were told the survivors list had only fifty names. A tense few moments. Then they heard our names were on it. All four names.

Patricia wrote, simply, "All in tears." There was no need to say anything more.

Lynn and I finished reading, and we both knew then what we had to do. We had to go south; we had to get right away from Nairobi and its memories of death and flaming destruction. We needed to be with members of our family in a place that was familiar.

But neither of us could bear the thought of flying. We were afraid we would crack under the strain. How would we persuade our sons to board an aircraft again after what had happened? I couldn't imagine how that could be achieved without disturbing scenes. Perhaps we could go by ship?

We discussed it with Lufthansa's passenger service manager Taj Gulam and by noon the next day it was all arranged: the airline would pay for our train journey to Mombasa and the sea voyage to Durban, in South Africa.

Ten days after the crash that had changed everything, a diesel locomotive pulled our train slowly out of Nairobi and headed east towards the Indian Ocean. Night had fallen and in the dark we clicked steadily past the aircrash site on the far side of the Mombasa road. A bank of red landing lights gleamed near the end of the airport runway. Beyond the lights there was darkness, nothing to see. But we knew what lay there, and stared silently into the African night until the last of the airport had slipped from view. Life's journey had ended in that field for fifty-nine fellow travellers; ours continued, winding its way on into the unknown. It was a strange and deeply moving moment.

A tremendous jolt woke us in the morning. The train came to a sudden stop. We leaped out of our bunks, hearts beating wildly, and I heard a locomotive horn sounding in alarm. We looked out of the window, but could see nothing but the wild African bush.

A railways official walking along the train corridor stopped to tell us what had happened. Two giraffe had stepped in front of the locomotive and had been killed. The impact had damaged the locomotive, so we would have to wait for a replacement to be sent from the next station.

"Where are we?" Lynn asked.

"Tsavo," the official said helpfully, smiling as he bent his tall body to peer out of the compartment window. "A very famous place."

He walked on, and we sat back, wondering nervously how good the traffic control was on the railway. The engine took two hours to arrive and we spent the time watching far-off buck through the haze, sitting in the heart of the Tsavo National Park. It would have been a paradise for tourists, but we were too shaken to appreciate it and half-expected another train to plough into the back of us. We eventually arrived in Mombasa three and a half hours late, but luckily the *SS Karanja* was still moored at the quayside and we sailed that evening.

A few days later a storm struck us in the Mozambique Channel. The ship rolled and shuddered. Spray pounded over the deck outside our cabin and in the lounge some joker remarked, "This ship is doomed!"

It was the worst thing anyone could have said. Our nerves were near breaking point. Despite taking tranquillisers, we couldn't sleep and spent a terrifying night listening to the creaking of the ship, feeling each sickening rise and fall as we headed into the waves.

The storm abated, we sailed on. A few hundred miles more, and we finally arrived, steaming into Durban harbour on a bright December morning, and there, waving from the top of the ocean terminal, were Patricia and Ian Horsfield. We had come a full circle: they had seen us off from the airport in Johannesburg nearly three months before and now they were the first to welcome us back.

As we stepped onto dry land, I swore never to travel anywhere again. But, deep down, I knew that would be impossible.

16 • *Flying again*

Almost without exception, the survivors had felt a compulsion to get away from the scene of the crash as soon as possible. But they discovered that leaving Nairobi did not end their suffering.

Back at home, they struggled to find ways of coping with their confused feelings. Some suffered for months, some for years from insomnia, nightmares, emotional distress, extreme nervousness, claustrophobia, depression, and a lack of judgment relating to size and distance.

Johannesburg businessman Manfred Wengerek had a strange experience. He was sitting in the first class section, three rows from the nose, on the starboard side, when the 747 struck the ground. Trapped between the seats after the long slide through the mud ended, he managed to pull himself free. He looked back as he struggled to his feet and realised the aircraft had broken apart in several places. Then he saw flames. He ran, managed somehow to find a way out, and jumped from the aircraft. As he did so, he heard a frightful explosion.

When he returned to Johannesburg after the crash, he decided that his office was too small and bought a huge factory. He and his staff moved in, but after a while he realised the building was ridiculously large, so he sold it and moved to smaller premises.

"I took a bit of a knock, lost a few thousand, but I had to get out of it," Manfred Wengerek said later. "I don't understand what made me act that way."

While Manfred Wengerek was considering the size of his office, in Britain survivor Terry Partridge was struggling to recover from the distress that had forced him to abandon his business trip to South Africa and return home.

A two-month course of sedatives prescribed by his doctor reduced the intensity of his symptoms. His condition gradually improved. Three months passed, and the moment came when he had to board an aircraft and fly again. After all that he had been through, this took a special kind of courage. His route was identical to the one he had been following when he crashed: Manchester to Frankfurt, and from there via Nairobi to Johannesburg.

From the moment he stepped aboard at Manchester, airline staff did their best to distract him, and by the time he reached Frankfurt to board the 747 to

Johannesburg, Terry Partridge had had so much to drink that he was not sure if he was on an aircraft or a bus.

He woke up after landing in Nairobi with "the worst hangover I've ever had in my life." Ahead of him was the take-off for Johannesburg. But the alcohol had anaesthetised him to the fears of the journey and helped him over that psychological hurdle. He flew on without a hitch and arrived safely.

Several more flights followed, and he managed to cope without breaking down. Once, while flying over Namibia, in south-west Africa, the aircraft passed through severe turbulence and he felt "very frightened indeed, my heart thumping like I've never experienced before."

When he was last in contact with the author, Terry Partridge reported that he had flown many thousands of miles around the world since his experience over Namibia and felt he had come to terms with his fears. As long as the flight was normal, he was not anxious, but he was still deeply affected by anything unusual, like flying through a storm, or being shaken about by turbulence.

Another who suffered was Gerd Kampf-Emden. He returned to Germany the day after the Nairobi accident with his gashed foot heavily bandaged. Two months later, he flew again, accompanied by his wife, taking the same route as the crash flight. This time the 747 landed safely in Nairobi, refuelled, then failed to restart.

Time went by. Gerd Kampf-Emden sat strapped to his seat, waiting. His nerves were taut. What had gone wrong?

The pilot's voice came over the public address system. Take-off would be delayed because of a defect in one of the engines. Repairs would take a while, but the journey would be resumed shortly.

It was too much for Dr Kampf-Emden. He got up and approached the Lufthansa crew, explaining that he had been in the *Hessen* crash and now felt extremely nervous about this flight. Would it be possible for him and his wife to transfer to another flight for the final leg of their journey to Johannesburg?

The airline staff were most understanding, and made arrangements. Half an hour later, the Kampf-Emdens boarded the incoming British Airways flight and took off for Johannesburg. They arrived safely and heard afterwards that the Lufthansa 747 had flown in about three hours late after an uneventful flight.

Four months after this incident, Dr Kampf-Emden was involved in a new drama at Nairobi. He was on board a British Airways jumbo bound for Johannesburg. After refuelling, the big jet thundered down the runway, the nose wheels lifted, and the jet rose sluggishly from the ground.

Dr Kampf-Emden felt an icy hand clutch at his heart. Something was going wrong again at Nairobi! The jumbo was not climbing normally. Like *Hessen*, it was flying parallel to the ground.

The pilot's voice broke in to inform passengers that he was having problems with one of the engines and would have to land.

Dr Kampf-Emden sat nervously in his seat as the jet struggled to gain altitude. Then it turned back and lined up for the landing approach. The jet dropped gently and coasted in over the grassy outfield. There was a bump, the wheels touched, and there was the shudder of reverse thrust. The 747 slowed and taxied back to the terminal building, where Dr Kampf-Emden stepped out of a defective aircraft for the third time in six months. He and his fellow passengers were booked into a hotel for the night.

After this third incident, Kampf-Emden said grimly, his colleagues had become superstitious and advised each other, "Never fly with Kampf-Emden. You are sure to run into trouble!"

Would he ever really recover from the trauma of the *Hessen* crash? He was not sure. "Even today, although I have flown often since then, I haven't got over the events of Nairobi," he reported. "I am extremely anxious during take-off and landing, because I know that these are the dangerous flight manoeuvres. I react very nervously and do not sit calm and collected in aeroplanes like I did in the past."

Back in Johannesburg, after our voyage down the east coast of Africa, Lynn and I and our sons struggled to recover a sense of purpose and bring some normality back into our lives. But it was difficult. We rented a flat, and our sons went back to school. I began working for the *Sunday Times*. Lynn began mastering the technicalities of a new camera; her previous one had gone up in smoke at Nairobi, along with all her European photographs.

Lynn and I tried not to think too much about what had happened, but it was impossible not to. People kept asking about the crash, so it was always there, in the background of our lives.

At home, acting out their darkest fears, the boys played bizarre games, building toy aircraft from Lego blocks, and hurling them down the stairs to see how many plasticine "passengers" survived. They pretended to burn paper aeroplanes. They seemed afraid of all forms of transport and, given the choice, preferred to stay at home and not go anywhere. At night, they could not sleep with the lights off. When they did sleep, they had nightmares, often waking in tears. Lynn and I did our best to comfort and reassure them, but we were still shocked ourselves, and our progress, as the months went by, was slow and gradual.

And then I was invited to fly again.

A publication in San Francisco asked me to travel to Nairobi to write a series of articles about the work of the UN Environment Programme.

Could I really do it? Could I fly again? I was not sure. My mind went back to the morning when we had all stood shaking in our muddy clothes on the slope outside Nairobi, watching the 747 burn. It had been impossible to believe that I would ever be able to board an aircraft again. The months had gone by . . . seven, eight, nine months, and now I had to decide.

Lynn said, "You should do it."

"Do you really think so?"

"Yes," she said. "It's important, and it'll be good for you to tackle a really big project again."

"But what about you and the boys?"

"We'll manage," she said. "It won't be easy. But it might be a good thing for us all if you fly off to Nairobi and come back safely."

So I contacted the editor and said, yes, I would write the series. But I was still not sure, and had several terrifying nightmares in those weeks before the flight: 747s nose-diving into the earth, or crashing on take-off and exploding in flames.

It did not help to explain the law of averages to our sons; they had been in an aircraft and it had crashed. As the day of the flight drew nearer, there were tears, sleepless nights and nightmares, and I seriously considered not going. Was it fair to put them through all this?

Then, one October evening, almost before I was ready for it, I was climbing the steps below the huge hunched shape of a Lufthansa Boeing 747. Destination: Nairobi. I entered the doorway forward of the wing and turned towards the tail. I had asked for the same port-side seat I had occupied on the doomed *Hessen*, on the aisle, between the wings, theoretically the strongest section of the jet. And there it was. Row 26.

It seemed strange to be buckling in again, seeing everything from the same seat, everything seeming so familiar, yet so alarming. The cabin crew had been forewarned about me, and did what they could. They smiled, they stopped by for a brief chat, they asked if I needed anything. They did everything except mention the crash.

But they soon left . . . and I was alone.

In fact, I had felt *alone* even while they were talking and being kind. Because they had no idea what it had been like. How a smooth, shiny, highly technical machine, with its smiling, glamorously groomed crew, could be transformed into something unimaginable in seconds, leaving passengers and crew clawing their way to safety through smoke, and fire and wreckage.

The jet began to move. We were taxiing slowly away

from the airport buildings. I was desperately reading the safety instruction sheet when I felt a terrible panic and had a sudden sick feeling that the jet would explode in flames. We were all so vulnerable, just little bits of flesh and bone.

The jumbo taxied to the head of the runway and the captain announced we were ready for take-off. My mouth went dry. I wiped the sweat from my face. The engine noise built up, the jet shook, and we were off. So slow, it seemed. There was a rushing, airy sound and the runway lights flashed by faster and faster. I had a cushion and blanket resting on my knees. My legs were braced, pushing against the floor.

The nose lifted, and I felt so nervous I thought I would be sick. The critical moment came. The main wheels lifted. I was sure we would crash back down. But we went on climbing, the engines whining steadily. Keep going, I breathed, keep going. My eyes were momentarily squeezed shut. The engines were thrusting us up powerfully through the night sky. When I looked again I saw stars, and through the porthole to the left, beyond two fellow passengers, the lights of houses, streets and vehicles were falling far below, growing smaller and smaller, until they became sparkling specks in the night.

The 747 eventually levelled off, but I could not relax. I kept glancing at my watch. Time passed so slowly. I tried to read, but couldn't. Each patch of turbulence was terrifying, and I flew the whole way with the seat belt fastened.

At about midnight I saw the lights of Nairobi glinting in the dark. The jumbo lined up, the runway appeared and we hurtled in from the night. The darkness came up to meet us. There was hardly a jolt. We touched down smoothly and rolled, and rolled, slowing.

I had made it, but I felt awful. I was drenched in sweat.

17 • *Coping with fear*

As the years have passed, the experience of escaping from the burning 747 at Nairobi has continued to affect the lives of survivors. A few have decided not to fly again. Others have changed career, or declined opportunities for advancement, in order to limit or reduce the hours they spend in the air.

Several of those who continue to fly do so only after developing strategies to help them cope with fear and anxiety. Despite outward appearances, time has not dulled the horror of that November morning. What has happened, for most survivors, is that day-to-day routines and the pressures of busy lives have forced us to live in the present. As a result, the events of the crash no longer dominate everyday thoughts and behaviour as much as they once did.

But none of us has forgotten. All it needs is for something to touch off a reaction. Like old soldiers at memorial services, who break down in tears at the sounding of *The Last Post*, air crash survivors react instantly and viscerally to booming explosions, low-flying jets, the shriek of tearing metal, the smell of burning plastic, and many other things.

Each survivor responds to the long-term emotional and psychological difficulties caused by an air crash in his or her own particular way. My experience of flying to Nairobi ten months after the crash made me realise that I might never overcome my fear of take-offs. But if I wanted to continue working internationally as a journalist, or visiting fascinating faraway places, I would have to fly . . . and that meant coping, somehow, with terrifying take-offs.

While I was strugggling with my fears, my wife Lynn was suffering from depression. This lasted for several years after the crash. She eventually recovered and, using tranquillisers to help with the anxiety she, too, experiences on take-off, she has since flown more than half a dozen long-haul journeys. Together, we have viewed the skyscrapers of New York, seen the Taj Mahal by moonlight, and eaten a sandwich in a park overlooking Sydney Harbour Bridge in Australia.

Being able to do this has not been easy. But, over the years, I have developed a method. I read all the facts about aircraft accidents, confronting the issues, rather than avoiding them.

For me, it is important to choose airlines and types of aircraft with a good safety record, and to sit between the wings, on an aisle, close to an exit. Once on board, I read all the safety material and map out several escape routes. But, despite all my preparation, each time I fly there is a moment when terrible memories take over my mind.

They begin the instant the cabin doors are sealed and the aircraft begins moving away from the airport buildings. Buckled in, the seat belt tight across my waist, aware of the faint smell of kerosene and the gentle bobbing motion as we taxi towards the runway, I try to calm myself by repeating the facts I know to be true: that flying is one of the safest forms of travel; that thousands of people are flying all over the world at any one moment; and that I have flown safely many times before.

Once I've done all that, it's almost time for take-off. I have to be a little trusting (or fatalistic). I know the statistics are in my favour: most flights reach their destination safely and without any serious difficulties. I know, as the roll begins, that I will once again be filled with nervousness and anxiety . . . but not for long.

Soon we'll be soaring high above the earth.

18 • *What happened*

Investigations began within hours of the accident and were conducted by the East African Community Accident Investigation Branch, assisted by two members of the United Kingdom Accidents Investigation Branch. Also participating were representatives of the states of registry and manufacture, and of the Boeing company and Lufthansa German Airlines.

Evidence was gathered from a variety of sources. The crash site was examined and the distribution of wreckage was plotted in order to reconstruct the crash sequence. The flight recorder was recovered intact, and investigators also had access to tapes from the control tower. Boeing ran tests on the wing flaps, the pneumatic system and its related warning lights. Finally, the cockpit crew were interviewed.

Lufthansa conducted an internal inquiry of its own and later dismissed the Commander, Captain Christian Krack, and Flight Engineer Rudi Hahn. The co-pilot, First Officer Hans-Joachim Schacke, was reduced in rank.

Supported by Vereinigung Cockpit, the German pilots' association, Krack and Hahn instituted a legal action against the airline for unlawful dismissal. Krack had, in the meantime, obtained a suspension from flying on medical grounds, which safeguarded his pension. The legal action was eventually ended by a compromise settlement.

The East African Community report was officially released in Nairobi in July 1976. A summary described the accident:

The aircraft was operating Lufthansa flight 540/19, a scheduled international passenger and cargo service from Frankfurt, Germany, to Johannesburg, South Africa, with an intermediate stop at Nairobi. During the take-off from Nairobi the crew felt vibration or buffeting after lift-off and suspected engine trouble. Subsequently the Commander, suspecting wheel imbalance, raised the landing gear.

The co-pilot, who was handling the aircraft, noticed a complete lack of acceleration and had to lower the nose in an attempt to maintain airspeed.

The aircraft lost altitude and the rear fuselage made contact with the ground approximately 1120 metres beyond the departure end of runway 24. Parts of the aircraft struck an elevated road 114 metres further on and it started to break up.

The main portion skidded an additional 340 metres, during which it turned to the left through approximately 180 degrees. The aircraft was destroyed by impact and subsequent fire.

The report reached the following conclusions:

FINDINGS

1. The crew were properly licensed and experienced.

2. The aircraft had been maintained in accordance with an approved maintenance schedule and its Certificate of Airworthiness was valid.

3. The weight of the aircraft and its centre of gravity were within the prescribed limits.

4. The aircraft took off with the leading edge flaps in the retracted position, with the result that it became airborne in a high drag, partially stalled condition.

5. The loss of ground effect during the climb-out, together with the probable presence of slight adverse wind sheer and the opening of the landing gear doors during the retraction cycle contributed to a further reduction in performance, with the result that the aircraft descended and struck the ground.

6. Following the introduction of a modified procedure which involved the closing of the pneumatic system bleed valves, the revision of the cockpit checklist after starting was completed did include a requirement for checking the re-opening of the bleed

valve switches, but did not specifically call for a check on the pneumatic system.

7. After the engines had been started the flight engineer omitted to open the bleed valves, thereby rendering inoperative the pneumatic system which powered the leading edge flap units.

8. The indications of the leading edge position prior to take-off could not be positively established. However, it is extremely unlikely that the flight engineer's annunciator panel indicated that all the leading edge flap units were in the correct take-off position.

9. In view of the inherent possibilities of incorrect leading edge flap operation and the critical nature of leading edge flap position during the take-off phase, adequate warning of incorrect position should have been provided. The existing indication system in use at the time of the accident did not meet this requirement.

10. Cockpit procedures did not call for any cross checking by the commander of items on the flight engineer's panel.

11. The accident could probably have been averted had the pitch angle been reduced and power been increased sufficiently early in the flight.

12. The pilots did not take effective recovery action in the short time available to them because they did not identify the semi-stalled condition of the aircraft

until alerted by the stall warning system shortly before the aircraft struck the ground.

13. The stall warning system did not give adequate warning of the critical condition of the aircraft because it was not programmed to take account of leading edge flap position. Had it been so programmed, its operation at lift-off might have alerted the crew in time to effect a recovery.

14. This accident was preventable. Inadequacies in international incident reporting procedures and effective follow-up action could be considered a contributory factor.

CAUSE

The accident was caused by the crew initiating a take-off with the leading edge flaps retracted, because the pneumatic system which operates them had not been switched on. This resulted in the aircraft becoming airborne in a partially stalled condition which the pilots were unable to identify in the short time available to them for recovery.

Major contributory factors were:

1. The lack of warning of a critical condition of leading edge flap position.

2. The failure of the crew to satisfactorily complete their checklist items.

RECOMMENDATIONS

It is recommended that:

1. The take-off configuration aural warning system programme on Boeing 747 aircraft should be modified to include leading edge flap position.

2. The take-off configuration aural warning system on Boeing 747 aircraft should be excluded from the list of allowable deficiencies.

3. Consideration should be given to the incorporation of leading edge flap position in the aircraft's stall warning programme.

4. Consideration be given to the inclusion of a pneumatic duct low pressure warning on the Pilot's Annunciator Panel.

5. Consideration be given to amending operating procedures where necessary to include a cross-check by the Commander of important items on the flight engineer's panel.

6. In Boeing 747 and similar aircraft, States of Registry should require the carriage of a multi-channel flight data recorder compatible with ARINC 573 or equivalent characteristic.

7. In Boeing 747 and similar aircraft, consideration should be given be given by States of Registry to require the installation and use of hot microphone cockpit voice recorder circuits during the take-off, approach and landing phases.

8. Implementation of adequate international incident reporting procedures, as initiated in the

Accident/Incident Reporting System (ADREP) of the International Civil Aviation Organisation, including effective follow-up action, should be enforced.

ACTION

The Chief Inspector of Accidents in East Africa took immediate action to alert world airlines as soon as it became apparent that the leading edge flaps had failed to extend prior to *Hessen*'s take-off on November 20.

On November 23, 1974, three days after the crash, following a request from him and the United States National Transportation Safety Board, the Federal Aviation Administration (FAA) recommended an interim flap inspection procedure. All Boeing 747 operators were urged to ensure that the flaps were extended to the normal take-off position before leaving the ramp and to get a qualified ground observer to make a visual check.

On December 6, 1974, the manufacturer telexed all Boeing 747 operators, briefly describing the circumstances of the Nairobi accident and emphasising the necessity for checks on bleed valve switches, leading edge circuit breakers and alternate system switches.

On December 11, 1974, the FAA issued a Notice Of Proposed Rule Making, proposing an Airworthiness Directive which would require modifications to the existing leading edge flap indication system, and the addition of an input from the leading edge flap logic unit to the take-off aural warning system.

On December 16, 1974, Boeing suggested alternative modification proposals:

a. that the amber light on the pilot's panel would illuminate when any one leading edge flap unit was not fully extended and the trailing edge flaps were at a take-off setting.

b. that the limit switches in the leading edge flap motors would cause inputs to the take-off aural warning system when any flap unit was not fully extended and the trailing edge flaps were at a take-off setting.

The FAA accepted these proposals and issued an Airworthiness Directive covering the modifications, effective from March 24, 1975. The Directive was to be complied with within five months.

COMPENSATION

The issue of financial compensation for survivors did not form part of the official accident report, but is worth mentioning here.

Survivors who lost clothing and luggage as a result of the accident were compensated, in excess of the international agreement, by Lufthansa within a few weeks. Several survivors who had been injured and relatives of those killed claimed damages from the airline's insurers. In many cases, settlements were negotiated.

In a later development, twenty-nine survivors, including both passengers and crew members, brought a group action against the Boeing Company, of Seattle, Washington, alleging negligence in the design, construction, production, manufacture, service, certification, testing, sale and inspection of *Hessen*.

The group further alleged that the aircraft had been "in a defective and unsafe condition, and unsafe and unfit for sale and use in the way and manner for which it was properly intended." The group claimed also that Boeing had been "negligent in failing to warn of known defects" in the Boeing 747 aircraft. Boeing strongly denied all the allegations and opposed the action.

The group action continued for some years before being resolved in an out-of-court settlement.

19 • *Those who died*

Abbott, Alan, 41
Assmann, Horst, 35
Assmann, Leone, 35
Assmann, Renate, 3
Behrmann, Boy, 69
Birth, Klara, 44
Braue, Günther, 39
Braue, Gustav, 76
Brodersen, Horst, 32
Broutschek, Hildegard, 61
De Candia, Francesco, 35
Eckert, Anette, 2
Eckert, Helga, 32
Fickenwirth, Karin, 34
Fickenwirth, Werner, 34
Fischer, Manfred, 34
Fischer, Petro, 27
Fitz, Bonnie, 4
Fitz, Heide-Marie, 33

Fitz, Nicole, 1

Frankenberg, Helmut, 44

Friedrichs, Harry, 63

Gabusi, Marco, 25

Galitzine, Marie (Maya), 44

Grant, Anthony

Hämmerle, Elisabeth (Sister Bona), 72

Haug, Gerhard, 47

Hohenleitener, Hilaria (Sister Blandina), 52

Isebeck, Dr Klaus, 38

Jäger, Lothar, 40

Kriegleder, Renate (stewardess), 24

Lauricks, Sibille, 37

Lockyer, Victor, 37

Maier, Theresia (Sister Annuntiata), 63

Malmquist, Lars, 29

Merrick, John (Paddy), 52

Nachtsheim, Helge (Mickey Mouse stewardess), 35

Nachtsheim, Klaus, 39

Nemitz, Joachim, 29

Nietser, Rolf (steward), 28

Panayotou, Stilianos, 24

Pantazopoulos, Ioannis, 48

Rönnfeldt, Reiner, 24

Schmidtsdorff, Dr Peter, 36

Schönhöfer, Resi, 69

Schwarzenberger, Martin, 32

Seegers, Wilhelm, 60

Seidel, Ernst, 58

Selbach, Rita (stewardess), 22

Setzer, Anna (Sister Richardis), 62

Skogberg, Kaj, 46

Smits, Hubert, 62

Solibakke, Alfred, 77

Solibakke, Veronica, 77

Stosch, Elke, 30

Teufel, Siegfried, 31

Vidal, Traude-Liese, 44

Vohs, Manfred (steward), 27

Zahn, Peter, 35

20 • *About this book*

When I began working on this book, I had a clear idea about the sort of book it should be.

It should be about people. It should describe as accurately as possible the experiences and feelings of passengers and crew members who were aboard Lufthansa's Boeing 747 jumbo jet *Hessen*, when it plunged back to earth after taking off from Nairobi Airport on that November morning many summers ago.

During my contact and interviews with fellow survivors, I was seeking answers to a number of questions that might produce a different response from each person:

What did it feel like to know that the aircraft you were flying in was crashing, that in seconds your life might be over? What thoughts flashed through your mind? How did you react?

These were difficult questions to answer, but almost without exception, those survivors I approached responded without feeling inhibited, and with an honesty and openness that was admirable. The result, in my opinion, is a book that goes beyond the usual news media reportage of air disasters. Thanks to the response of my fellow survivors, readers are able to *feel* the turmoil and shocked disbelief that passengers experienced, and to share vicariously the panic and desperation as they struggled to find a way out of the burning wreckage.

I am grateful, also, for the contributions from those people who were not on board the aircraft, but watching as it struck the ground and burst into flames. In some cases, these people ran to the scene to help, at great personal risk. It is difficult to read some of these accounts without being moved to tears.

I have a special word of thanks for those who relived the nightmare of waiting at airports and other places to hear the fate of family members and friends. In some cases, the ordeal they lived through lasted for several days, and their suffering was as stressful and mentally draining as that of the accident survivors.

Although this book is mainly about people, it has been necessary to give some technical details in order for readers to understand what went wrong and why the jumbo jet crashed. The details given are based on the official report of the East African Community Accident Investigation Branch, a copy of which was secured for me by the Community's Chief Inspector of Accidents, Mr D C Stewart, in Nairobi. I was also fortunate in having the advice of Andrew Wilson, aviation writer for *The Observer* in London.

Tracking down fellow survivors and witnesses was a major task. I was assisted by my wife Lynn, who set aside her own photographic work and writing in order to help complete this project on time. She spent many hours transcribing taped interviews, researching, comparing notes, inputting and encouraging. For this revised edition, she has, in addition, handled all the design work for the book itself and for its wider marketing presence on the internet. My thanks, love and gratitude.

Many people helped to create this book. I am particularly grateful to the following: John and Jean Bing, Dancy Bruce, Kay Cokayne, Mr D C Stewart of the Accident Investigation Branch, East African Community, Mother Dietlinde Geis, Rudi Hahn, John Hall, Colonel M J Harbage of Nairobi Hospital, Mr J L Beecher, consultant surgeon at Nairobi Hospital, Tillie Harmel, Hermann Hennecke, Erich Hesse, Gisela Hutton, Bruce Hobson, Margaret Hooker, Patricia and Ian Horsfield, Robert Horsfield, Squire Horsfield, Gino Iannibelli, Karl, Renate and Nancy Kahn, Dr Gerd Kampf-Emden, John Kingsley-Heath, Bob Laburn, Jimmy Laing, Jock and Betty Leslie-Melville, Carol Mall, Hans Neeb,

Joseph Odiyo Onguru, Peggy Ottenheimer, Jill and Terry Partridge, Tom Scott, Hans-Joachim Schacke, Edmund and Elinor Senkler, Henriett Smith, Malcom Solts, Manfred Wengerek, Andrew Wilson, Stephen and Elke Day.

Looking back at the events of the world's first Boeing 747 crash, I am aware that there are several people whose personal courage and sense of duty played a crucial role in allowing me and my family, as well as many other passengers, to escape from the burning aircraft. I would like to express my thanks and gratitude to steward Tom Scott, stewardess Evelyn Rehm and an unidentified male passenger, whose combined efforts managed to force open the emergency exit in front of the starboard wing.

Few of us will forget the sensation of leaping through that open space, onto the escape chute, and the sudden realisation, as we fled, that we might now survive, despite all that had happened.

Earl Moorhouse, Bath, England.
March 2013

The Author

Earl Moorhouse was born in London and travelled to South Africa with his parents at an early age. He spent part of his childhood in Port Shepstone and lived later in Pretoria, where he began working as a newspaper reporter during the apartheid years. He returned to England in 1970.

During a colourful and eventful journalistic career he has worked in England, South Africa and Australia, and undertaken assignments all over Europe and in Kenya. In the 1980s he was appointed Editor of the Somerset Guardian series of newspapers in England.

He is the author of two books: *Wake Up, It's A Crash!* and the autobiographical novel *The Last Summer In Little England* based on his experiences of growing up in a small South African seaside town in the 1950s.

Earl and his wife Lynn live in Bath, Somerset, England.

Earl and Lynn Moorhouse with their sons Brendon, aged six, centre left, and Garett, aged seven, centre right, at the Hilton Hotel, Nairobi, after the accident. Picture: Daily Nation.

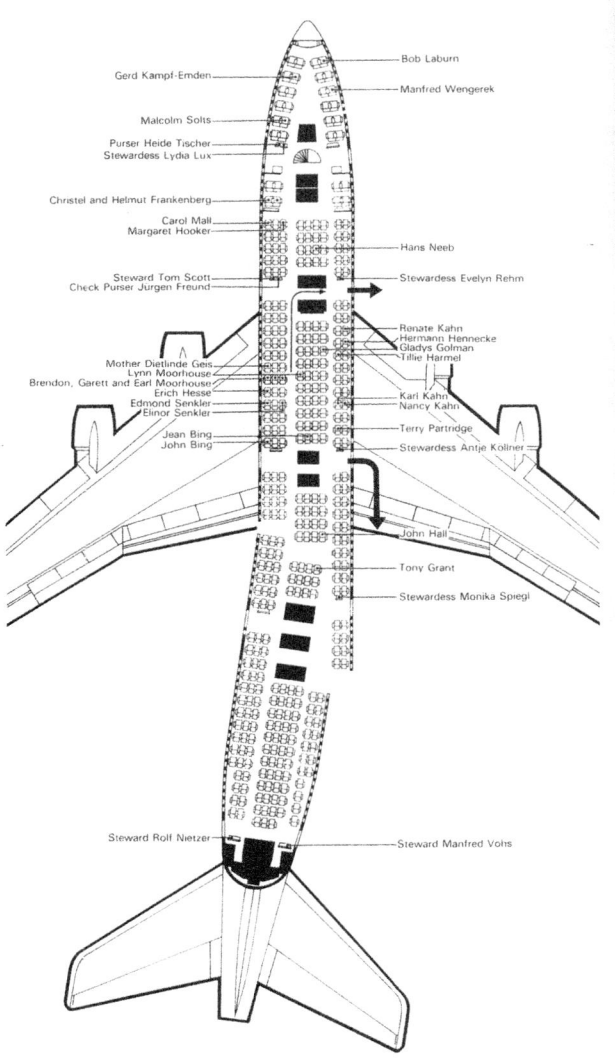

Bob Laburn

Gerd Kampf-Emden

Manfred Wengerek

Malcolm Solts

Purser Heide Tischer
Stewardess Lydia Lux

Christel and Helmut Frankenberg

Carol Mall
Margaret Hooker

Hans Neeb

Steward Tom Scott
Check Purser Jurgen Freund

Stewardess Evelyn Rehm

Renate Kahn
Hermann Hennecke
Gladys Golman
Tillie Harmel

Mother Dietlinde Geis
Lynn Moorhouse
Brendon, Garett and Earl Moorhouse
Erich Hesse
Edmond Senkler
Elinor Senkler

Karl Kahn
Nancy Kahn

Terry Partridge

Jean Bing
John Bing

Stewardess Antje Kollner

John Hall

Tony Grant

Stewardess Monika Spiegl

Steward Rolf Nietzer

Steward Manfred Vohs

- 257 -

A dramatic photograph of the burning Lufthansa Boeing 747 dominates page 1 of The Standard newspaper published in Nairobi on November 21, the day after the 747 crash. The edition carries the corrected death toll of 59 and highlights the fact that 98 people survived. But not all survivors escaped down emergency chutes. Some clawed their way to safety through cracks and holes in the burning fuselage.

For its special edition, published only hours after the Lufthansa Boeing 747 crashed, Nairobi's Daily Nation featured this remarkable photograph taken by staff photographer Samuel Ouma, who was at Nairobi Airport to record the arrival of a West German Government delegation. Ouma's picture was taken shortly after the aircraft struck the ground and burst into flames. It shows rescue workers and others running towards the crash site.

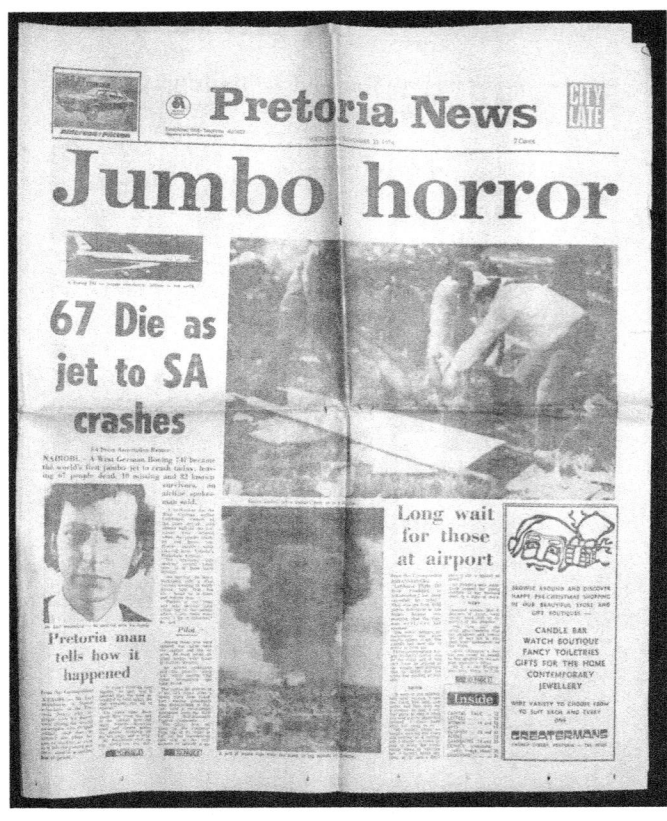

The front page of the Pretoria News edition which appeared on the streets a few hours after the Boeing 747 crash. The death toll given as 67 is incorrect and was later corrected. Note story lower left, headlined Pretoria Man Tells How It Happened, which was based on an interview with author Earl Moorhouse shortly after he and his family had escaped from the burning aircraft. He worked for the newspaper for several years before leaving on the journey that ended with the crash at Nairobi.

A spread of photographs published in The Standard newspaper, Nairobi, shows all that remained of the wrecked Boeing 747 after the initial fire had been brought under control.

Index

**The Last Summer in Little England
by Earl Moorhouse**

Transported from England to a small town on the sun-drenched South African coast by his parents a few years after the end of World War II, an English boy finds himself living in what some people call Little England. But it doesn't look at all like England. Here there are Zulus, Afrikaners, witchdoctors, monkeys, snakes . . . He also has to contend with a recently acquired stepfather, shell-shocked in the war.

   This funny, delicate and sensitive book appeals on several levels, moving the reader with its childhood view of the adult world and its deep sense of loss and longing. A story that is amusing, nostalgic, and at times achingly sad.

What some reviewers have said:

'I couldn't put it down. A delightful book, with every word conjuring up a sense of being there.' - Your Books

'Goodness, I so enjoyed this book. It is riveting reading . . . one of those special books about South Africa's darker days that remains with you . . . poignant, touching and rather sad, but at the same time, it is funny and quirky.' - Rivergirl

'A pleasant must-read for all those who, if nothing else, at least once in their lives called South Africa "home"!' - Reshaad M Hussain

Squire's Yard

Available from Amazon worldwide.

**Aunt Coco And The Marionette Man
by Lynn G Moorhouse**

Photographer Elle revisits the days when she was growing up in an unconventional, free-thinking English family living in South Africa in the years after the Second World War. The photographs on her living room wall evoke a time when people dressed up and went dancing on Friday nights, travelled on mailships and steam trains, and occasionally swam naked in farm dams.

Elle and the letters from her Aunt Coco tell the story of the bi-sexual Leo (Elle's father), whose sometimes eccentric behaviour creates bewilderment and tensions within the family. Both Leo's, and his sister Coco's tolerant outlook are increasingly at odds with the repressive government and the laws covering "morality".

What reviewers have said:

'*No other novel I have read this year has impressed me on so many levels.*'

'*If I could give this book a six star I would . . . it is just stunning.*'

'*This is not just a book you read - it is a book you feel.*'

'***An outstanding, literary novel of deep complexity.***'

'*Truly fantastic storytelling.*'

Available from Amazon worldwide.

Printed in Great Britain
by Amazon

58514835R00159